GRACIOUS
CHRISTIANITY

GRACIOUS
CHRISTIANITY

LIVING THE LOVE
WE PROFESS

DOUGLAS JACOBSEN AND
RODNEY J. SAWATSKY

Baker Academic
Grand Rapids, Michigan

© 2006 by Douglas Jacobsen

Published by Baker Academic
a division of Baker Publishing Group
P.O. Box 6287, Grand Rapids, MI 49516-6287
www.bakeracademic.com

Second printing, June 2006

Printed in the United States of America

Library of Congress Cataloging-in-Publication Data
Jacobsen, Douglas G. (Douglas Gordon), 1951–
    Gracious Christianity : living the love we profess / Douglas Jacobsen
    and Rodney J. Sawatsky.
        p.   cm.
    Includes bibliographical references (p.   ) and index.
    ISBN 10: 0-8010-3139-7 (pbk.)
    ISBN 978-0-8010-3139-7 (pbk.)
    1. Theology, Doctrinal. 2. Love—Religious aspects—Christianity.
I. Sawatsky, Rodney. II. Title.
BT78.J34 2006
230—dc22   2005022551

for

Rhonda Hustedt Jacobsen
and
Lorna Jeanne Sawatsky

who display graciousness in all they do

Contents

Preface

This book was written by two friends who, over the past few years, have become soul mates in their thinking about Christian faith and life. This does not mean we agree on everything, though we do agree on a lot. Friendship goes much deeper than agreement. It reaches down to the most basic levels of loyalty, faithfulness, and trust. Friends are willing to let one another be who they are, but they also encourage one another to a higher plane of living. Perhaps most of all, friends speak truthfully to one another.

It is that last part—speaking truthfully—that applies most to this book. This is our attempt to discuss the challenges of Christian faith in today's world in as straightforward and honest a manner as possible. It is virtually certain that we are not right all the time, and we are sure you will disagree with us on some point or another. But we hope this book will prompt your thinking and cause you to reflect on your own beliefs about God, the world, others, and yourself.

Our goal is to engage you in conversation, not just conversation with us but conversation with other Christians who hold views different from your own and conversation with some of the great Christian thinkers and writers of the past. This is a short book, so that conversation can only begin here, but we hope it helps you think about your own religious com-

mitments and encourages conversations that are congenial
and productive.

Using a book to start a conversation has its challenges. In
a book, the authors always have the first word, and readers
just have to follow along. There is no back and forth exchange;
everything is rather one-sided. What is more, certain passages
may unintentionally come off sounding rather dogmatic, as
if you had better not disagree with us on those points if you
know what is good for you.

But, of course, you can disagree with anything in this book.
In fact, we welcome your responsiveness. To help things along
in that regard, a variety of questions for reflection have been
scattered throughout the book. Some of these questions were
raised by colleagues, friends, and students who read earlier
drafts of this work and helped us refine the text in light of
their queries and critiques. Other questions represent our own
continuing uncertainty about how best to express some of the
things we are trying to say. You will undoubtedly bring yet
more questions to this text. Because of that, we suggest that
you read this book with someone else or with several other
people so that all of these questions, both ours and yours,
can be discussed out loud.

If you do that, you may discover that you surprisingly agree
with some people you never would have imagined agreeing
with and you disagree with some people with whom you
thought you shared a common worldview. You never know
what might happen in a good conversation. But the best thing
that can happen in any conversation is always the same:
Somewhere along the way you realize that your conversation partner has become a friend.

Our own conversation began eleven years ago. At the
time, Douglas Jacobsen (Jake to those who know him) had
been teaching at Messiah College for ten years, and Rodney
Sawatsky had just come to the college as president. Our life
histories were rather different. Jake had been raised in and
around New York City, while Rod hailed from the farmlands of
Canada. Rod had deep roots in the Dutch-Russian Mennonite

community, while Jake was eclectically evangelical. But our paths had begun to converge long before we met. Our academic training was similar—a mix of theology, sociology of religion, and history—but more than that, our Christian visions of the world had begun to bend in the same direction. We both had been pondering how Christians could be more embracing of those different from themselves yet remain people of strong faith and conviction.

It did not take long to discover our common perspectives and interests. During the last ten years, we spoke frequently about faith and life and the vocation of being Christian scholars. Those conversations touched on many topics, but they often wound their way back to concerns about our students. What elements of the Christian faith will help them be agents of salt and light in the world after they graduate? What genuinely motivates students, or anyone else, to devote their lives to service, leadership, and reconciliation in church and society? What kind of education might best facilitate maturation in the areas of character, intellect, and Christian faith?

It was not simply our students we had in mind. We are both fathers, and we care deeply about the legacy of faith we are passing on to our children, who are now adults in the early stages of their independent lives and careers. They were raised in the church and teethed on the stories of the Bible, but as mature adults, they have new questions about the connections between historic Christianity and contemporary developments in science, politics, the arts, business, medicine, religion, and culture. How does Christianity sustain their desire to love God, seek the common good, serve those in need, and celebrate life?

As teachers, we have become fairly adept at providing answers to students when they ask faith-related questions. Most ministers develop the same ready-answer skills. But whether a professor, a college president, or a pastor, when our own children ask questions of faith, the responses often take on a different tone. When we talk with our own children, pat answers to difficult questions do not suffice (even if those simple answers are sometimes absolutely true). Instead, we speak from the heart as honestly and truthfully as we can, because that is what they expect and deserve, and because they will know right away when we are fudging.

Many of our own children's questions stem from observing the defensiveness and mean-spiritedness that pervade so many expressions of Christian faith in America and around the world. They realize that many other religious groups have also become more extreme, even violent, in the ways they press for or against social change. But because they themselves are Christians, they are most disturbed by the attitudes of other Christians. It can be tempting simply to quit talking about religion, to follow the old adage that polite conversation avoids religion and politics. But a failure to converse about matters of faith perpetuates ignorance, freezes personal development, and leaves us with nothing but stereotypes of one another.

We are convinced that the good news proclaimed by Jesus, when it is properly understood, will never foster hateful faith but will make us gracious instead. Christians acknowledge Jesus as their model, and accordingly, they seek to mimic, as much as is humanly possible, the love Jesus exemplified in all he did. To our way of thinking, ungracious Christianity is a contradiction in terms, an oxymoron. Gracious love defines the core of God's character, and gracious love defines the life and work of Christ. The more we understand that and the more we let those truths seep into our souls and color the way we see ourselves and others, the more gracious our Christianity will become.

Just as we began writing this book, Rod was diagnosed with a very aggressive form of brain cancer. Because Rod was so truly in love with life, news of his cancer hit him hard. But he was not about to let go of life without a fight. He had two surgeries, endured several rounds of chemotherapy, and took whatever other steps seemed helpful or necessary. His type of cancer is, however, currently incurable, and Rod always knew that someday it would take his life. His main concern as death approached was not for himself but for those around him, especially for his wife, Lorna, and his three daughters Tanya, Lisa, and Katherine.

When faced with this kind of terminal disease, people typi- KEUBLER-cally go through a sequence of responses that include shock, ROSS denial, anger, despair, and finally acceptance. Rod did not follow that pattern. In particular, he never got angry at God for his sickness. Such anger is predicated on the assumption that faith in God is supposed to make our lives easier. However, Rod did not see things that way. He never doubted that God loved him, but he also never assumed that God's love was supposed to render him or anyone else exempt from the pain and suffering of ordinary human life. Instead, God's grace provides strength to bear the sorrows of life with dignity, peace, hope, and grace. Rod displayed those virtues in the way he lived and in the way he died.

Rod's death occurred as the final pages of this manuscript were being completed. His theological and academic insights pervade the manuscript, and his pastoral concerns have deeply shaped its contents. While Rod was exhilarated by scholarly pursuits, his real passion was always for people, all kinds of people. He liked to say that faith is a verb, not a noun. Faith is more relational than rational. Especially, faith is incarnational. It exists in people—in flesh-and-blood people who hug those they love and who laugh and cry and die—much more than it exists in the abstract truth of any theological proposition. This does not mean doctrines and dogmas are inconsequential. It just means that faith goes beyond them.

The week after Rod learned he had cancer, he distributed a Lenten sermon to the Messiah College community that he had delivered at a church in Lancaster, Pennsylvania, the previous year. The title was "The Broken Body of Christ," and Rod remarked that his disease had placed him in a new situation to reflect on the reality of Christian hope in the midst of brokenness. Here is an excerpt from that sermon:

Why are we here tonight? . . . Let me suggest that we are here tonight not because we are the good folk of Lancaster, Pennsylvania, not because we are the righteous ones, not because we have all the answers. Rather, we are here for the very opposite reason. We are here because we recognize our humanity, because we are very aware of our limitations, because we know our own deep brokenness, because we admit we are people in need.

And we are here tonight for another very important reason. We are here because we know that God knows. God knows us precisely for who we are. God identifies with us fully and completely. God has become one with us, united with us in our weakness, in our limitations, in our brokenness. This is the wonderful message of the Christian gospel—God becoming human, the Word made flesh, the spiritual assuming the physical, the embodiment of the divine. God is not distant and separate from us. Rather, God is very near and one with us. . . .

The incarnation means that God in his very own body knew what it meant to be human, to be limited, to be broken—to be one with us. This embodiment of God is surely the greatest mystery and glory of our faith—indeed, of history. . . .

God is embodied not only in Jesus Christ. . . . We, too, are the body of Christ. You and I are the body of Christ. The church present and future is the body of Christ. The church is surely the broken body of Christ. It is so broken, so fractured, so riddled with humanity's foibles and follies that we wonder if we can even call it the body of Christ.

Jesus already in his day saw all this division and prayed to his Father that we might become one with one another and one with him, even as he and his Father were one. He prayed in this way because he was concerned that our divisions would undermine the message, that the world would not believe because of our hostilities. . . .

Like Jesus, Paul longed for the unity of the church. But such a unified body of Christ will become a reality only if everyone in the church worldwide listens very carefully to these words: "I beg you to live a life worthy of the calling to which you have been called, with all humility and gentleness, with patience, bearing with one another in love, making every effort to maintain the unity of the Spirit in the bond of peace." Humility, gentleness, patience, love—these surely are the very opposite of the judgmentalism and self-righteousness that characterize so much of Christianity. Paul begs us to recognize that we all are broken, all are sinners. Only when we know ourselves as the broken body of Christ, where humility, gentleness, patience, and love give evidence to our brokenness, will we live a life worthy of the calling to which we have been called and thereby become the triumphant body of Christ.

We are here because we humbly know we are a broken people and because we thankfully know that God in Jesus was also broken with us and for us.

Our hope, Rod's and mine, is that this book, despite all its weaknesses, will in some way help those of us who call ourselves Christians to be more gracious in the way we live, acknowledging our own brokenness and reaffirming our commitment to the humble, gentle, patient, and loving way of Jesus.

Introduction

What Is Gracious Christianity?

W e have a gracious gospel. The good news that Jesus proclaimed is that God is graciously disposed toward us. God loves us, and, indeed, God loves everyone and every good thing in this wonderful world in which we live. We are expected to do the same. The gospel invites us to mimic God's own graciousness in our lives. It calls us to become so enveloped in God's graciousness that we become conduits of God's grace and love for others. Graciousness is a nonnegotiable dimension of Christian faith. It goes to the very core of the gospel. It is what makes the gospel good news.

Defining Terms

The terms related to the word *grace* (including *graceful* and *gracious* and their various derivatives) play an important role in Christian faith, but the meaning of these terms is not always clear. In the *Oxford English Dictionary,* three pages are needed to explain the twenty-eight meanings attached to the single word *grace.* The words *gracious* and *graceful* require another two pages or more. The meanings of the word *grace* include "the quality of producing favorable impressions," a "sense of duty or propriety," and "prayer said before meals," but in this book the term is linked much more closely with the eleventh meaning in the dictionary: "the free and unmerited favor of God as manifested in the salvation of sinners and the bestowing of blessings." *Grace* describes the experience of receiving God's love.

As for *graceful* and *gracious*, these adjectives are sometimes equated with style and fashion, indicating that someone has "a pleasing or attractive quality" or is socially refined and "endowed with charm." These adjectives can also signify beauty, elegance, and poise. Those are all good traits, but in this book we mean something different when we use the words *graceful* and *gracious*. The kind of gracefulness and graciousness we have in mind is a response to God's love. Graciousness is how we externalize to others the grace we have internalized from God.

Graciousness understood in this way focuses on kindness, compassion, and friendship rather than on mere attractiveness or elegance. People who are truly gracious are attractive, but their winsomeness transcends merely skin-deep beauty. Theirs is an attraction based on goodness. This is the kind of attraction that Mother Teresa possessed. Mother Teresa was far from beautiful in the glamour-magazine sense of the word, but she was clearly one of the most attractive people in the world because of her moral beauty and compassion for the poorest of the poor in Calcutta's slums.

◆ ◆

Who are the most graceful or gracious Christians you know? What makes them stand out as examples?

◆ ◆

In many ways, *grace* and *love* are synonyms. To be gracious toward someone is to show that person love, but graciousness points toward love with an important qualification. Graciousness is love that never forces itself on anyone. Sometimes people almost love us to death, smothering us with their love. Usually these people genuinely care for us, but they cannot differentiate between welcome love and over-bearing love. They intrude in our lives with good intentions but negative results because they pay no heed to whether we really want their help or not.

Gracious love is different. Such love does not intrude but stands ready to help only when it is appropriate, desired, and needed. When love is given graciously, it preserves our dignity and never makes our neediness public. In a sense, graciousness could thus be defined as love offered truly lovingly, as love that makes no show of itself, as love that seeks no praise in return.

That, of course, is precisely the kind of love we have received from God, and when we understand the gracious nature of God's love for us, the only appropriate response is to love other people in the same way. And that is what we mean by gracious Christianity. It is Christianity so deeply rooted in God's love that we cannot help but love others in the same gracious way. It is cause and effect. The love and grace we receive from God are refracted through our lives and redirected toward others.

People who are truly gracious also welcome the love and care given by others. Graciousness is about being on the receiving end of love as well as on the giving end. In this sense, grace and graciousness point toward community and sociability and toward nurturing relationships among people. Gracious Christians recognize that others can be conduits of God's love to them just as they can be messengers of God's love to others.

Overcoming Ungraciousness

While all Christians are called to be gracious, none of us is as gracious as we should be. We get grumpy. We snipe at one another. We are sometimes downright nasty. This should not be the case, but it comes as no surprise. Christians are imperfect. We are sinners who still need to be fully redeemed.

We are works in progress, but thankfully God is still active in our lives slowly making us better. Someday, by God's grace, we will become the people we were meant to be.

The goal of becoming more gracious as Christians is not, however, a matter of simply waiting for God to change us. The Christian life rarely works that way. Instead, we are called to cooperate with God's will for our lives, and we are called to actively strive to live up to the standards to which God has called us.

◆◆◆◆◆◆◆◆◆◆◆◆◆◆◆◆◆◆◆◆◆◆◆◆◆◆◆◆◆◆◆◆◆

Is graciousness merely a synonym for simply being nice? How much graciousness can we realistically expect from one another? Does being gracious mean we must avoid confrontation and shun all debate? Can a person be blunt and gracious at the same time?

◆◆◆◆◆◆◆◆◆◆◆◆◆◆◆◆◆◆◆◆◆◆◆◆◆◆◆◆◆◆◆◆◆

But how do we do that? What is the pathway toward becoming more gracious followers of Jesus? Some would say the answer is simple: just do it. The Bible gives us the guidance we need: turn the other cheek, go the extra mile, forgive others when they harm us, be patient with everyone. In short, start acting more graciously right now, and with time and practice, graciousness will become a lifelong habit.

There is wisdom in that advice. If we genuinely commit ourselves to do something over and over again—in this case, to practice graciousness in all our daily encounters with others—it can eventually become second nature. Great athletes and musicians do this all the time. Dribble a ball long enough or practice the piano often enough and you can almost do it in your sleep.

But practice alone is not always enough; sometimes we need more. For example, while all dieters try to change their eating behaviors, those who are most successful are usually the ones who also change the way they think about food and feel about themselves. Concentrating merely on behavior is not enough; we also need to pay attention to emotions and ideas.

Learning to live more graciously as Christians necessarily involves changing our behavior, for graciousness is expressed in the way we live. But becoming more gracious also requires changing misconstrued thoughts and feelings about God, the world, and other people. It is difficult to treat others with grace if we feel emotionally ill-disposed toward them; it is next to impossible to treat others with respect if our theology says it is all right to disdain them.

How do you think doing, believing, and feeling should relate to each other in the Christian life? Is one of these—thinking, feeling, or acting—more important than the others in your own life? Are they sometimes in tension with each other?

While the pathway toward greater graciousness in Christian faith and life involves behavior, emotions, and ideas, this book focuses primarily on the realm of ideas. Some practical comments about behavior are included, and some emotional connections hopefully will occur along the way, but the main concern is with the ideas that form the framework for living the love we profess. Within the realm of faith, this kind of framework of belief is called theology.

A Theology for Gracious Christianity

This book is a theology for gracious Christianity. It is a concise but relatively comprehensive overview of what most Christians have believed about God, the world, themselves, and others for most of the past two thousand years, explaining how those beliefs encourage and support graciousness in faith and life.

While the subject is theology, we have tried to keep this text largely free of theological jargon. This book is written in plain English. Some theological texts are highly technical, and professional theologians have no need to apologize for using specialized language in their publications; such practice is common in every academic field of study. But theology is not just a discipline for specialists. All Christians are to some degree theologians, and this book is designed to be a resource for them.

Though written in plain English, this book is intended to make you think. While comprehensible, it is not necessarily simple, and it is certainly not simplistic. Thinking through the implications of faith is challenging work, and it takes effort to evaluate the world intelligently and to reflect on the meaning of the Christian message. Sometimes it is easier simply to repeat old answers without analyzing them, but graciousness requires thoughtfulness, self-awareness, and empathy. If our faith is true, knowing what we believe and why will ultimately increase our ability to listen to others with genuine fairness, respect, and compassion.

The Jesus Creed

The heart of gracious Christianity is Jesus' dual commandment to "love the Lord your God with all your heart, and with all your soul, and with all your mind, and with all your strength" and to "love your neighbor as yourself" (Mark 12:30–31). Theologian Scot McKnight has recently labeled this double rule of love the "Jesus creed," and he argues that it is "the foundation of everything Jesus teaches about spiritual formation."[1]

◆◆◆◆◆◆◆◆◆◆◆◆◆◆◆◆◆◆◆◆◆◆◆◆◆◆◆◆◆◆◆◆◆◆

Are you familiar with any other creeds? How is the Jesus creed similar to or different from these other creeds? Does the Jesus creed capture the essence of Jesus' life and teaching?

◆◆◆◆◆◆◆◆◆◆◆◆◆◆◆◆◆◆◆◆◆◆◆◆◆◆◆◆◆◆◆◆◆◆

McKnight is not alone in grasping the importance of this "creed." People from all over the theological spectrum are making the same point. For example, Rick Warren, who is a conservative Christian and author of the enormously popular *Purpose Driven Life*, writes, "The point of life is learning to love—God and people. Life minus love equals zero."[2] Speaking from a rather different location on the theological spectrum, the liberal biblical scholar Marcus Borg echoes Warren and McKnight. Borg calls Jesus' dual commandment to love God and our neighbors the "great relationship," and he says that this "remarkably simple vision" of life with God and others is the "center of a life grounded in the Bible."[3]

This book takes the Jesus creed, this simple but profound core of Christian faith, and uses it as a lens to examine the various subject areas of theology. The eight chapters of this book describe what this creed has to do with:

- how we understand God and creation
- what it means to be human
- how God speaks to us
- what salvation entails
- what the Spirit does for us
- why the church exists
- how to read the Bible
- what will happen in the future

Looking at these topics from the perspective of the Jesus creed does not change the message of historic Christian faith. Instead, it refurbishes our theology, like polishing a tarnished silver tea set helps restore its original luster. Polishing a tea set does not change the shape of anything. Everything is still in the same place—spout, handle, feet, and lid—but the dullness is gone, and it shines like new. Polishing our Christian beliefs with the soft cloth of God's love can help us renew our ways of thinking in a similar way.

Generous Orthodoxy and Gracious Christianity

Love of God and neighbor has always defined the heart of Christianity, but the need to reaffirm this truth visibly and vigorously is especially urgent today. Mean-spiritedness and hate are on the rise in both America and around the globe, and religion is often implicated. Instead of acting as a restraint, religion is sometimes the cause of tension, tirades, and terror. The title of Charles Kimball's recent book *When Religion Becomes Evil* aptly captures that mood. Many

♦ ♦

What are some examples of religion becoming evil? Is it easier to discern evil looking back in history than in current events? What are warning signs that religion may be becoming evil?

♦ ♦

expressions of religion are becoming more strident and shrill, including some expressions of Christianity.

Seeing this, many contemporary Christians feel a need to recover a broader and deeper orthodoxy that can keep evil more consistently at bay. Brian McLaren, in particular, has suggested that we need a more "generous orthodoxy," and he says that this new style of orthodoxy will have to be formulated in the language of both/and rather than either/or. Thus, the rather lengthy subtitle of his recent book is "Why I am a missional + evangelical + post/protestant + liberal/conservative + mystical/poetic + biblical + charismatic/contemplative + fundamentalist/calvinist + anabaptist/anglican + methodist + catholic + green + incarnational + depressed-yet-hopeful + emergent + unfinished Christian."[4] McLaren's plus signs serve as symbols of a faith that unites rather than divides and acknowledge how much we can learn from each other.

A generous Christian orthodoxy uses the Bible as its primary source and is also informed by tradition, reason, and experience. These four sources of theology are sometimes called the Wesleyan quadrilateral, but they apply to the dynamics of any Christian theology. All Christians share the Bible as their primary authority in matters of faith and life, and all Christians also appeal to tradition, reason, or experience to make their points. Tradition can take many forms. Most often we think of the creeds or confessions of faith that we recite in our churches, but tradition also includes the songs we sing, the ways we worship, the passages of Scripture we find most helpful, the ministries of service and compassion we render to others, the Christian writers we find most compelling, and many other aspects of faith that have been handed down to us and that we are passing along to others. Reason refers to what seems logical to us and what seems blatantly illogical; it also involves the coherence of our ideas, which is an important consideration in most theology. Experience includes both specifically religious experiences (such as a dramatic conversion or the lack of such an experience) and more general life experiences (such as cultural or ethnic identity, gender, the type of work one does, and family characteristics). All these dimensions are integrated into our theological thinking, because theological thinking is holistic.

The particular way of understanding gracious Christianity in this book is not the only way to think graciously about faith. Our views are limited by our own experiences and reasoning abilities and will be modified, augmented, and corrected by the insights of others. Our views are also shaped by our own traditions. While

What place does the Bible, tradition, reason, and experience play in your own theology? How would you rank these items in terms of their influence on your theology?

we draw from the broad history of Christianity (including Catholic, Protestant, and Orthodox perspectives), we freely admit that our own spiritual roots are Anabaptist, Pietist, and Wesleyan. This means, among other things, that we are committed to peace as a gospel imperative, to faith as necessarily lived in community, to the importance of a personal relationship with Christ, and to a spirituality that emphasizes justice and ethical decision making.

The gracious Christianity we wish to encourage in this book is not, however, specifically Anabaptist, Pietist, or Wesleyan. The adjective *gracious* is one that all Christians can adopt. The world needs gracious Christians of every kind: gracious Baptists as well as gracious Lutherans, gracious Mennonites as

well as gracious Presbyterians, gracious Catholics as well as
gracious Methodists, gracious Orthodox Christians as well as
gracious Pentecostals. Adding graciousness to our differing
self-definitions is not meant to blur honest differences. It is
meant, rather, to remind us how much we hold in common
as followers of Jesus and how much we share a commitment
to love God and to love our neighbors as ourselves.

Christians currently account for almost one-third of the
world's people, two billion out of a global population of just
over six billion. If the faith professed by those two billion
Christians became even a little more gracious, the dynamics
of the world community could be changed dramatically for
the better. Before it is public, however, gracious Christianity
is intensely personal. We are compelled to be gracious because we have been loved so graciously by God and because
we have been loved by others—the love of God usually flows
to us through others. Gracious Christians participate in that
cycle, giving back a small portion of the grace received from
both God and others. The graciousness we funnel back into
the world is only a fraction of the grace we have received,
but God can use small things to accomplish great goals. In
fact, God has for the most part chosen to change the world by
layering small grace upon small grace, and living graciously
as Christians allows us to assist in that work.

I

God and Creation

The Christian story begins with God as Creator and the world as creation. Our lives are enfolded within a vast and magnificent domain, and gracious Christianity is rooted in a natural sense of gratitude and awe. We are not our own makers. We are dependent on forces beyond ourselves, and we exist interdependently with everyone and everything around us. We are living in someone else's world. Our natural response, when these thoughts cross our minds, is reverence.

But Christians do not stop there. It is not simply creation that astounds us but the Creator behind the creation. Who is the Creator? What kind of God would do this? Why did God make the universe? Why and for what purposes did God make us?

The God Who Made the World

God did not create the world out of need or necessity. Rather, God made the world out of generous, self-giving love. Everything in the world exists because God loves it, and God's deepest will for the world is joy in the presence of its loving Creator. People do not often think of God as creating the world for joy and enjoyment, and Christians certainly do not always live in joyful awareness of God, but the Westminster Catechism gets it right when it says that our chief end and purpose is "to glorify God, and fully enjoy him forever." Christians worship a God who desires our deepest well-being and, indeed, our joy.

God created the world beautiful and good. In fact, the account of creation in the first chapter of Genesis says that after God created the world, God looked at everything that had been made and said it was not just good but *very* good. The God who created the universe—the God who gives life to all the plants and animals and single-celled creatures that live on the earth, the God who loves every human being who walks this planet—is a God who does things *very well*.

The God who created the world is a God who delights in wonder, beauty, and joy. When God made the world, all those qualities of life were braided into the very fabric of the universe. There is now no getting them out. It is true that sin and evil have deformed God's creation, making the world we live in far from perfect. But however much we mess things up, truth, beauty, and goodness can never be fully eliminated from this world.

Is it surprising to think of the world as made for joy? Do you set aside time to celebrate life's goodness? How much do you think evil has deformed the world? How much goodness is left?

Some versions of Eastern Orthodox theology suggest that for God to create the world, God first had to voluntarily shrink back a bit from filling all reality in order to make space for the world to exist. God scrunched back, like people in a crowded elevator, clearing a space for something else to enter.

This way of speaking about God is metaphorical. God is spirit and does not literally take up space like a physical object. Therefore, God cannot literally shrink in order to make room for the world. But the image is winsome, and, like any good metaphor, instructive. In the act of creation, God graciously invited something else to exist—something entirely new, something different and distinct from God's own self. In an act of stunning humility, God stepped back to allow space for the world to blossom into being.

Although the notion that God somehow shrank to make room for creation is an image that does not come directly from the Bible, it is in keeping with how God later underwent a process of "self-emptying" in order to squeeze into human existence in the person of Jesus of Nazareth (see Phil. 2:6–8). Both acts bespeak God's extraordinary graciousness in accommodating us. In fact, the essence of graciousness is the accommodation of others, and God modeled that in creation long before God required it of us.

The world did not, however, spring into existence all on its own simply because God opened a space where that could happen. Creation required God's active involvement. The book of Genesis says that God spoke and only then did the world begin to be. This image of God speaking the world into existence is, like the notion of shrinking, a metaphor. But in a vivid way, it depicts God as the life-giving source of the universe.

The Bible's description of creation is poetic, couched in the language and thought forms of people living in the ancient Near East. It addresses the deep issues of the world's meaning and purpose and provides only sketchy information, at best,

How do you understand the relationship between science and faith? How much or how little science do you think is included in the Genesis story of creation?

about the mechanics of how the world came to be. The Bible's scientific implications have, however, become a hot topic in many churches, communities, and school boards across the country. Some Christians claim that the Bible can be used to judge scientific data about the creation of the world, and, unfortunately, they sometimes make those claims in an angry and ungracious way.

Fertile and friendly conversation can take place between science and faith,[2] but science is a form of modern scholarship, and Christians are still trying to figure out how the older language of the Bible relates to this relatively new field of human inquiry. Sometimes Christians may need to oppose certain uses or tentative conclusions of science. For example, this was clearly the case during the early 1900s when the so-called science of eugenics asserted, following the laws of evolution, that the weaker members of society should be sterilized or allowed to die so that the human species as a whole could advance more quickly. Such thinking is utterly at odds with a Christian commitment to care for those who most need our help. But Christians welcome knowledge obtained through ethical scientific research, including information about the origins and development of the natural world.

The real importance of the Genesis creation narrative is found not in its scientific details or lack of such details but in the claims it makes regarding the character of the Creator and the underlying nature of the creation. Genesis tells us that God gave life to the world as a free and wonderful gift. Existence is a blessing. God created the world out of love and for the purposes of love. This positive perspective—a loving God who forms a delightful world—is what makes the Christian view distinctive.

The One and Only God

Christianity teaches that the God who created the world is the only God who exists. Like Jews and Muslims, Christians are radical monotheists. Because of that, Christians avoid calling God their own. God does not belong to us; rather, we belong to God. And the God we belong to loves the entire world. The one and only God of the universe transcends our narrow loyalties, and when we seek to follow that God, we are inevitably stretched in the process.

God is different and bigger and better than we are. This led Karl Barth, one of the twentieth-century's greatest theologians, to refer to God as the "Wholly Other."[3] God is so much bigger and better than we can imagine that all our little boxes of understanding deconstruct when we try to force God into them. Several millenia ago, the writer of Isaiah depicted God as saying, "My thoughts are not your thoughts, nor are your ways my ways. . . . For as the heavens are higher than the earth, so are my ways higher than your ways and my thoughts than your thoughts" (55:8–9).

Because God is Wholly Other, some Christians have adopted a style of talking about God that focuses on how much we do *not* know rather than on what we know. This is sometimes called apophatic theology or negative theology. The term *negative theology* may grate on our ears, but negative theology makes an important point: Nothing we can say about God comes close to capturing the awesomeness of God's being. Moreover, our propensity to talk too much about God can get us into trouble. Human beings, including many Christians, are prone to refashion God in their own image. We want a pliable God who does our will, so we reenvision God in ways that fit our tastes. In the process, God's glory is often diminished and God's character distorted. Negative theology critiques these images we fashion for ourselves and suggests that silence about God may often be more appropriate than overly eager speech.

Historically, however, most Christians have felt it necessary and worthwhile to

♦ ♦

How much do we know about God? How much do we need to know? What are the most important things you would claim to know about God?

♦ ♦

try to describe God in a positive manner, even if none of our words can adequately describe God's full perfection, splendor, and beauty. In this kind of positive theology, the focus is on what we can validly affirm about God. So, for example, Christians have rightly said that God is the Creator. God is our Savior. God is omnipotent, omniscient, and holy. God hears our prayers; indeed, God hears the prayers of all people. And God judges justly.

Positive theology seeks to distinguish between better and more accurate ways of speaking about God and ways of speaking that may, in one way or another, partially misrepresent who God is. For example, to call God "king" misses the fact that God is also our friend and lover. The notion of kingship all by itself is too hierarchical and authoritarian to stand alone, since it does not capture these other more intimate aspects of how God relates to us. On the other hand, to call God simply a friend does not do justice to God's awesomeness and transcendence. No single word or image will ever suffice, which is why the Bible uses so many images to portray God's character and attributes.

In evaluating the language of positive theology, many factors come into play, including intelligent biblical interpretation and logical thinking, but there is also a practical test that seems to apply. The New Testament says quite bluntly, "Whoever does not love does not know God, for God is love" (1 John 4:8). If that is true, it seems like a good idea to assess what we say about God in light of this rule of love. Views about God that encourage us to love others are more likely on target than those that cause us to hate others or to hold them in disdain. An accurate view of God will never diminish our love for others.

The Trinity

Christians are monotheists who believe there is one God and one God alone. Yet, historically, Christians have also been trinitarians. The Trinity describes a threeness that exists within God's oneness, a threeness of Father, Son, and Holy Spirit bound inseparably together.

God's threeness is reflected, in some way, in the threefold activity of creation: God made the world, God sustains the world, and God will ultimately fully redeem the world and make it perfect. Christians often associate the original act of creation with God the Father, the ongoing work of sustaining the world with the Holy Spirit, and the process of redeeming the world with the Son.

But that way of speaking about God and God's activity in the world divides things up too much. In fact, Christians have historically said it is wrong to ascribe one action to the Father and another to the Spirit or the Son. When God acts, all three persons of the Trinity act together. Thus, the Spirit and the Son are involved in creation, and the Father and the Son have a role to play in the work of sustaining the world, and the Father and the Spirit are involved in redemption.

Christians often use the personal language of Father and Son to refer to the first two persons of the Trinity because this language portrays so powerfully the indissoluble, family-like bonds that hold the Trinity together. The point of using the language of Father and Son is not to describe God as male. The Bible includes many descriptions of God that are feminine along with masculine ones. Obviously, Jesus was a male, but God is clearly beyond gender. The language of Father and Son is a metaphorical way of describing the degree of intimacy that exists among all three persons of the Trinity.

How do you picture God? What images of God do you have in mind when you pray? In what ways does God seem male, female, or beyond gender? Do you focus more on God the Father, Jesus, or the Holy Spirit?

Over the centuries, Christians have struggled to understand the Trinity. Everyone has agreed that the full mystery of the Trinity is beyond human comprehension, but in the long conversation of Christian faith, some descriptions have been affirmed while others have been rejected as unhelpful or simply wrong.

Among the rejected options is a position called modalism. Modalists believe the threeness of God is like water, which can exist as ice, liquid, or steam. The external form, or mode, of the water changes, but the molecular substance of the water remains the same. Similarly, God can appear externally to us as Father, Son, or Spirit, but internally God is always the same and never changes. When first suggested, modalism seemed like a reasonable analogy of God's threeness in oneness, but it was eventually rejected for two important reasons. First, it is an impersonal analogy with the potential to misrepresent the dynamic and personal reality of God. God is not a thing but a person. Second, modalism implies that the trinitarian character of God is really a matter of shape-shifting. If we followed this analogy literally, we would reach the conclusion that God can exist only as one person of the Trinity at any given point in time. Since Christians believe God has always existed as both three and one, the water analogy, along with all similar shape-shifting analogies, was jettisoned.

One explanation of the Trinity that eventually was embraced by the mainstream Christian movement is the famous analogy of love developed by Augustine. Augustine, who was bishop of the city of Hippo in northern

◆◆◆◆◆◆◆◆◆◆◆◆◆◆◆◆◆◆◆◆◆◆◆◆◆◆◆◆◆◆◆◆◆◆◆◆◆

Some people think Christians are polytheists who worship three gods rather than one. How would you explain the Trinity to someone who thought that?

◆◆◆◆◆◆◆◆◆◆◆◆◆◆◆◆◆◆◆◆◆◆◆◆◆◆◆◆◆◆◆◆◆◆◆◆◆

Africa (present-day Algeria) during the early 400s, said that the act of loving another person always involves three components: a lover, the person who is loved, and the love that the lover feels for the beloved. For love to be real, he argued, all three elements must be present. Applied to the Trinity, Augustine said, God the Father is like the lover, God the Son is like the beloved, and God the Holy Spirit is like the love that binds the lover and the beloved together.[4]

Augustine's analogy of love is not perfect—no metaphor or analogy ever is—but it is helpful because it reflects the personal nature of the Trinity and affirms the simultaneity of God's threeness and oneness. It is also valued because it makes sense of the New Testament declaration that God is love. This is a somewhat odd statement. The Bible does not say that "God loves," which is what we might expect, but rather that "God *is* love." What could it possibly mean for God to *be love* and not merely to *be loving*?

Augustine's analogy explains how love can be the essence of God's being. Love always involves reaching out to others. God reaches out to us in love in much the same way we love others. But Augustine says that long before God's love became extended to others, it already existed in infinite intensity within the Trinity itself. Love is what holds the Trinity together. It is what makes the threeness of God a singularity. The trinitarian God literally *is* love. Love is not merely one personality trait among others that describes a part of who God is. Love defines the essence of God's being, a love that God extended to the world in creation.

While love is clearly central to who God is, what other character traits would you include in a description of God? How do these other traits relate to the idea that God is love?

Practical Implications of the Trinity

While people like Augustine made every effort to explain things clearly, the language of the Trinity can still become quite confusing, especially when debated by theologians. Theological debates are often important, but they involve a great deal of technical language that can sound like gibberish. Because of that technical language, the British writer Dorothy

Sayers worried that people in the church pews might conclude
that "the Father is incomprehensible, the Son incomprehensible, and the whole thing incomprehensible. It's something
put in by theologians to make it more difficult—it's got nothing
to do with daily life or ethics."[5] Sayers sympathized with those
who were confused by complicated theological debates, but
she rightly insisted that Christians still need to understand the
theological implications of the Trinity. Indeed, the language
of the Trinity has very much to do with daily life and ethics.

Let's start with ethics, the study of right ways of living.
Virtually all Christian ethics are ultimately grounded in an
understanding of God's character. The Bible says that we are
to be perfect as God is perfect (see Matt. 5:48), and that means
we are to model our way of living after God's own existence.
But what exactly does that mean? The Trinity gives us an
answer.

The Trinity tells us that part of the perfection of Christian
living is mutual, self-giving love. Just as the members of the
Trinity are bound together in love for one another, so we are
called to love those around us in the same unreserved and
uncalculating way. Especially within the church, where we
share life in the Spirit, we are called to mutuality of love. We
are to love and serve others, and, just as importantly, we are
to let others love and serve us when we need their help. We
may not do this very well, but it is the ideal. As Christians,
we strive to be a community in much the same way that God
as Trinity is a divine community of persons. Far from being
unrelated to life, the doctrine of the Trinity is the defining
core of Christian ethics.

Another tremendously important implication of the Trinity
has to do with epistemology. Epistemology is the branch of
philosophy that focuses on how we know what we know. Most
of us do not spend much time thinking about how we know
what we know, but theologians do. Especially when it comes
to knowledge of God, theologians want to know where good
ideas come from.

What the Trinity contributes to Christian epistemology is a reminder to be holistic. Because the Creator of the world, the Redeemer of the world, and the Sustainer of the world are all one and the same God, what we learn about God from creation (if we understand it properly) ought to correspond to what has been revealed about God through the life and work of Jesus (if we understand Jesus properly), and that, in turn, ought to correspond to what we believe about God from the experience of the Holy Spirit in our lives (if we understand that experience properly).

In other words, the development of a Christian understanding of the world, a Christian

> ◆
>
> How have your beliefs about God been shaped by your understanding of creation, your understanding of Jesus, and your understanding of the work of the Holy Spirit in your life? On which do you rely most heavily? On which do you rely the least?
>
> ◆

epistemology, involves a triangulation process much like that used in navigation. Global positioning devices use three satellites to tell us where we are. It is the same in matters of faith. God's trinitarian relationship to the world as Creator, Sustainer, and Redeemer provides three necessary points of reference.

Paying attention to these three aspects of God's relationship to the world allows us to navigate our way through the world intelligently as Christians. If we listen only to the voice of the Spirit in our lives, we may develop a truncated view of Christian faith and a partially distorted view of God. If we depend only on the revelation of God in nature, the same thing can happen. And even if we look only at Jesus as the basis of our faith and ignore the rest of creation and the work of the Spirit, we run the risk of having a limited and mistaken view of God, ourselves, and the world. It is only by holistically examining God's relationship to the world, by knowing God in trinitarian perspective, that we protect ourselves from developing a lopsided or unbalanced view of God.

Many complex issues need to be considered when discussing God and creation, and as a result, we may not fully agree on all the details. But two things are clear: God is love, and God's love for the world is expansive and embracing. The more we understand the depth of God's love, the more we ourselves will be able to love the world and everyone in it.

2

Human Nature

Peple are a very special part of creation. The author of
Psalm 8 says that human beings are made just "a little
lower than God" (v. 5). Genesis 1:26–27 says that we
are made in the image and likeness of God. While God loves
the whole world and everything in it, we—all of us who have
ever been born—occupy a special place in God's heart.

Our special status as bearers of God's image brings special
responsibilities. In particular, we are called to use our gifts
and talents in the service of God, in helping others, and in
caring for the natural world. We are here to play a positive
role in the created order, but we have not always performed
very well. Instead of serving God, we often serve ourselves,
and instead of looking out for the best interests of the world
and the people in the world, we often look out for our own
benefit and forget about everyone else. Therefore, questions
naturally arise: What kind of people were we created to be?

What went wrong? How are we supposed to treat one another? What is our true calling in life?

The Image of God

One of the oldest Christian explanations of the image of God (or *imago Dei*) comes from the Eastern Orthodox tradition, which links the image of God with freedom and rationality. Like God, human beings can think and decide and act. We are not mechanically determined machines, nor are we driven by instinct alone. We are people, and, as such, we possess the freedom and the responsibility to determine who we will be.

Individuals do not possess unfettered freedom. We are creatures, and we have limitations. Our biology and life histories have provided us with different sets of gifts and talents and with different burdens to bear. Some of us are healthy, while others must deal with debilitating diseases. Some of us are bold; others are relatively timid. Some of us have people who depend on us for their daily needs, while others have fewer direct responsibilities for others and can thus act more independently. Some people are born into wealth with apparently endless life options; others are raised in poverty and struggle just to scrape by. The range of our freedom is deeply shaped by many factors beyond our control: by the nations into which we are born; by the actions of our friends, neighbors, and enemies; by political structures that empower or oppress us; by the level of education available to us; by our genetic makeup.

At times, our lives are made easier by these factors, but sometimes our lives are made more difficult. Regardless of who or what has influenced us, however, we are ultimately responsible for what we do with our lives.

♦♦♦♦♦♦♦♦♦♦♦♦♦♦♦♦♦♦♦♦♦♦♦♦♦♦♦♦♦♦

What factors beyond your control have accentuated your freedom? What factors have narrowed the life options that are open to you? Is a person with a wider range of choices more likely to make wrong decisions?

♦♦♦♦♦♦♦♦♦♦♦♦♦♦♦♦♦♦♦♦♦♦♦♦♦♦♦♦♦♦

The choices we make decide who we become. Even if our choices are never absolutely free, they are still our choices, and no one else can make them for us.

The Bible describes the fundamental character choice each of us faces as a decision between "the way of life" and "the way of death." This choice is starkly framed in the book of Deuteronomy when God says, "I call heaven and earth to witness against you today that I have set before you life and death, blessings and curses. Choose life so that you and your descendants may live, loving the LORD your God, obeying him, and holding fast to him" (30:19–20).

The options of life or death are both open to us, and God asks us to choose life. God wants us to choose life. In fact, God is continually calling us, inviting us, and luring us to choose life, but God does not make that choice for us. God may intervene, nudging us one way or encouraging us in a different direction, but God does not dictate. God never takes over the strings of our lives and makes us dance like puppets to a tune we do not want to hear. Why? Because, from the start, God made us for freedom. God wants us freely to choose the good and creatively to embody that good in the way we live. Most of all, God made us free so that we can freely choose to love the God who gave us life.

Can you identify some points in your life when you were choosing between the way of life and the way of death? Were these dramatic moments of decision where the ramifications seemed clear, or were they subtle and understated, seeming almost inconsequential at the time? Do choices always require conscious reflection, or do our habits also reflect choices we have made?

Freedom, Failure, Dignity, and Doubt

Choosing the way of life is not necessarily easy. As a result of our own decisions and the decisions of those who have lived before us, the natural terrain of the world is now tilted against our ability to choose the good. It is hard to live in ways that are consistently holy and good. And it is frustrating that we often fail, even when we are trying to do what is right. The apostle Paul confessed that sometimes he could not make sense of his own actions, since "I do not do what I want, but I do the very thing I hate" (Rom. 7:15). All of us have experienced similar failures of character. Freedom of choice can result in sorrow and regret.

Yet freedom is to be cherished, nonetheless, and the freedom of others, especially those who cannot defend their own rights, needs to be protected. People are still people even if they have lost, or have never had, the ability to make decisions for themselves. Everyone bears the image of God and deserves respect because of that fact. The Bible speaks frequently about the need for those in positions of power to defend the rights of the oppressed and to preserve the dignity of the poor. Appropriate treatment of those on the margins of society is central to our faith: Christians strive to help those who need assistance and to treat all people with the respect due to equals.

Human freedom is a gift from God, so it can never be utterly destroyed. Even in the most trying circumstances—whether someone is deathly ill, a refugee, imprisoned, or abused—people maintain a spark of power to fashion a response. Still, in all too many instances, human freedom has been crushed to the point of being nearly extinguished. Every act of torture is thus not merely a crime against humanity but also an insult against God because it seeks to destroy part of God's image. Every incident of genocide is an evil directed against both God and humankind. The fact that people who participate in such acts sometimes say they believe in God—sometimes even call themselves Christian—is difficult to comprehend.

Coercion regarding matters of religious faith can be just as disturbing as political coercion. Faith can never be imposed on someone else: It is the voluntary response of an individual to God. Even the slightest hint of spiritual coercion should set off alarms. Attempts to threaten, cajole, pres-

sure, or trick people
regarding matters
of faith can result
in merely external
compliance rather
than internal con-
viction. As a result,
freedom to doubt
must necessarily be
respected as a part
of the freedom to
believe.

♦ ♦

How has the misuse of freedom caused sorrow or regret in your life? Where is human freedom most threatened today? Is Western-style
freedom—the freedom to do whatever one
pleases—the same thing as the freedom that
is a part of being created in God's image? Have
you ever seen religious faith imposed on people
or doubt disallowed?

♦ ♦

Love, Justice, and Common Humanity

A person who freely believes in God wants to live in a way
that pleases God, and Jesus clearly summarized what God
desires. First, we ought to love God with our entire being,
and, second, we ought to love our neighbors as ourselves
(Matt. 22:37–40). For Jesus, these two commandments were
inseparable.

When Jesus voiced this great law of love—the Jesus creed—
he was not being particularly original. The Jewish rabbi Hillel
had said much the same thing before Jesus began to preach.[1]
Thus, Jesus was not intending to provide the world with an
utterly new insight. Instead, he was underscoring something
that we already know deep within us: We are connected to
one another; our actions affect one another for good or ill;
we are not isolated individuals.

Writing in the eighteenth century, John Wesley, the founder
of the Methodist movement, appealed to this same law of
love, explaining it in the more modern economic language
of comforts, needs, and emergencies. He said:

We want everyone to love us, respect us, and treat us fairly,
mercifully, and truthfully. It is reasonable for us to expect them

to do all the good for us they can without harming themselves. According to this rule . . . their surpluses should be directed to our comfort, and their comforts to our needs, and their needs to our desperate emergencies. . . . Let us live by the same rule. Let us do to all people as we want them to do to us. . . . Let your surpluses give way to your neighbor's comfort. (Who would then have any surplus remaining?) Let your comforts give way to your neighbor's needs, and your needs to their desperate emergencies."[2]

Rather than being extraneous to human nature, this rule of love and compassion is deeply rooted in our souls. It is part of how we were made, and following it leads us into a fuller way of being human, more intense fellowship with God, and richer fellowship with one another.

We are relational creatures, and we need one another. In fact, this is so much the case that some theologians speak of relationality as the key characteristic that makes us human. They see relationality as part of the image of God. If we are free and reasonable persons, and everyone else is similarly free and reasonable, we are inseparably linked to one another through our choices. What we do affects others, and therefore we have to take others into account in our decision making.

Love and relationality define the deep reality in which we live, and Christians have traditionally affirmed that these creational values of love and relationality derive from the character of the Creator. Thus, the early twentieth-century Anglican theologian Evelyn Underhill could write in her book *The School of Charity,* "God is Love, or rather Charity; generous, out-flowing, self-giving love. . . . To enter the Divine order then, achieve the full life for which we are made, means entering an existence that only has meaning as the channel and expression of an infinite, self-spending love. This is not piety. It is not altruism. It is the clue to our human situation."[3]

The poet John Donne said much the same thing when he memorably penned the words "no man is an island . . . [but] each a part of the main."[4] Each of us is born into and raised within the context of family, community, and nation. As we grow older and mature, we join still other groups and communities, and we live within those expanding networks of relationship. We are not isolated individuals but persons in community who can enrich or impoverish the lives of those around us by our actions. The American educator Ernest Boyer summarized this vision of life by saying that "to be truly human, one must serve."[5] He believed service to others was both the highest expression of our freedom and the deepest acknowledgment of our human interconnectedness. When we voluntarily serve others, we are simultaneously doing what is best for us and what is best for those around us.

Historically, Christians have believed that we become whole persons through healthy relationships with God and others. Because of that, Christians have always felt a need to nurture families, churches, local communities, and the larger civil society—all the different contexts in which we learn how to live with one another—so that these varied social locations

What qualifies as service? Does it have to be unpaid volunteer work? Or can we serve through paid jobs and routine activities?

become and remain places where healthy relationships are possible and where human dignity is protected.

Human relationships are nurtured through expressions of both charity and justice. While love as charity stresses individual efforts on behalf of others, the ideal of justice focuses on the social and the communal. Justice is not limited to helping others in their need but also involves changing social structures so that those needs themselves might be lessened or even eliminated.

The Catholic ethicist Thomas Massaro contrasts the social orientation of justice with the personal character of charity: "Where charity tends to involve individuals or small groups of people acting to meet the immediate needs of others, work for justice involves a more communal and even global awareness of problems and their potential long-term solutions. Where the notion of charity calls to mind voluntary giving out of one's surplus, the notion of justice suggests there is an absolute obligation to share the benefits of God's creation." Massaro goes on to say that "we need not choose between justice and charity. Rather, we can seek the best way to combine heroic acts of love with a clearheaded view of the importance of justice that must be regularized and routinized in fair institutions that respond to the needs and dignity of all."[6]

◆◆◆◆◆◆◆◆◆◆◆◆◆◆◆◆◆◆◆◆◆◆◆◆◆◆◆◆◆◆◆◆◆◆

Groups like Amnesty International and the International Justice Mission raise awareness of global injustice, and missionary agencies, charities, and newspapers inform us of the needs of our local and international neighbors. How do you decide where to get involved?

◆◆◆◆◆◆◆◆◆◆◆◆◆◆◆◆◆◆◆◆◆◆◆◆◆◆◆◆◆◆◆◆◆◆

To be truly Christian and to be genuinely human coalesce. We all need to be loved. We all need, at one point or another, to help someone else or be helped in return. We all want to be treated fairly and respectfully. Thus, we should not be surprised to discover that what Christians see as good, proper, and laudable is often the same as what most other people see as good, proper, and laudable. Writing to the Galatians, Paul acknowledged as much, noting that no law forbids the character traits Christians value most, such as love, compassion, and kindness (5:22–23). While these virtues are distinctively Christian, Paul indicates that they are not *uniquely* Christian. Other people share those values, and Christians, accordingly, celebrate them whenever they are exemplified in anyone's life.

Sin and Sorrow

While love and justice define the ideals of human behavior, we all know that love and justice are often in short supply. As human beings, we frequently fail one another. Many of these failures stem from simple stupidity, immaturity, and mistakes of judgment. We do not mean to harm anyone, but we sometimes harm others anyway through our obliviousness and thoughtless behavior. At times, however, another element prompts our failings, and that element is sin.

Sin is anything that willfully diminishes the life that we and the rest of creation are meant to enjoy. Sin is living against the grain of God's universe. Sin can take many forms, expressing itself both in action and in the choice not to act when action is called for. In some people, sin springs from unwarranted pride; in others, it is a matter of pathological self-deprecation. In some cases, sin is aggressive and bold; in others, it is timid and self-effacing. In some instances, sin is premeditated; in others, it is almost totally spontaneous. Sometimes sin is crass and rude, and sometimes it is thoroughly cultured and polite.

Whatever particular form it takes, sin always involves a choice to prefer ourselves over others, over nature, and over God. It is rooted in the desire to follow our own way regardless of the consequences. Quite obviously, this means sin always works against genuine love and justice, but, less obviously, sin also works against the best interests of the sinner. In the book of Jeremiah, God accuses the people of Israel of having "forsaken me, the fountain of living water, and dug out cisterns for themselves, cracked cisterns that can hold no water" (2:13). That is exactly what sin is like: It draws us away from the true source of our being and ultimately gives us nothing in return.

Sin is self-defeating. We need others, and we need God, and sin cuts us off from both. But we lapse into sin anyway because it has such powerful short-term appeal. The temptation to sin is always, in some sense, a lie. It beguiles us away from the truth of God and the truth of who we are. But unfortunately, people believe that lie again and again. People who are not Christians fall for it, and so do Christians.

When we sin, we are accountable for what we have done, especially for how our sin affects others. Catherine of Sienna, who lived in the fourteenth century and is considered one of the greatest theologians in the history of the church, said, "There is no sin that does not touch others, whether secretly by refusing them what is due, or openly by giving birth to the vices."[7] Our sinful actions harm us, but they also deeply wound others. Sin causes pain. Sin promotes anger, bitterness, and strife. Sin can crush people by taking away their will to live or their means of survival. Sin sows distrust and destroys relationships. Sin undermines life.

The reality of sin is why repentance, restitution, and forgiveness are also necessary aspects of the human condition whether we are Christians or not. When we sin, we need humbly and honestly to acknowledge what we have done and to ask for forgiveness from those we have sinned against. If something has been stolen, it should be returned. If we have lied about something, we should tell the truth. If we have slandered someone, we should help restore that person's reputation.

But sometimes the consequences of our sinful actions are not reversible. It is not always possible to undo the damage we have done, and that is part of the tragedy of human life. Regret and remorse cannot necessarily reverse the consequences of our wrongful actions and attitudes.

♦♦♦♦♦♦♦♦♦♦♦♦♦♦♦♦♦♦♦♦♦♦♦♦♦♦♦♦♦♦♦♦♦♦

Do you know someone who lives with regret over past sin? Do you know someone who lives with bitterness over a wrong done to them? Does forgiveness happen at a particular moment, or is it a process?

♦♦♦♦♦♦♦♦♦♦♦♦♦♦♦♦♦♦♦♦♦♦♦♦♦♦♦♦♦♦♦♦♦♦

We have all been wounded by these kinds of irreversible sins, and those who have been wounded the most need our special support and care.

Forgiveness is part of the human condition. Sometimes it is easy to forgive, especially when people are truly sorry for what they have done. But at other times, forgiveness seems almost impossible, especially when the pain is great or when people refuse to acknowledge how much they have hurt us.

Yet forgiveness is ultimately necessary in order to move beyond bitterness and to preserve our own humanity. The only alternative is to live with a shrunken spirit and a diminished sense of what it means to be human. As Alan Paton, the South African activist and author, has written, "There is a hard law. . . . When an injury is done to us, we never recover until we forgive."[8]

All of this—love, justice, freedom, service, sin, repentance, and forgiveness—is part of what it means to be human. It is part of how God has made us. Being a Christian does not lift us above the human condition. Rather, it calls us to participate in life in a new way—in the way of Jesus, following the way of life. Should we ever forget our own humanity and think of ourselves as separate from or better than the rest of the world, we can easily become ungracious in the way we treat others. Christian teaching, however, calls us back to reality. We are all created in God's image. We all need to be loved, and we need to love others. We all want to be treated fairly. We all also fail one another from time to time and need to be forgiven. Remembering all that—remembering our common humanity in all its complexity—is one of the most important keys to living graciously as Christians.

Hearing God's Voice

God wants to be known, and because God wants to be known, God speaks to us. In fact, God is speaking all the time. Psalm 19 says, "The heavens are telling the glory of God; and the firmament proclaims his handiwork. Day to day pours forth speech, and night to night declares knowledge" (vv. 1–2).

But how do we hear God's voice, and what does God say? Does God communicate with us like a lecturer doling out information, or is God's voice more personal than that? Who can hear God's voice? Does God speak to all people or only to Christians? And what kind of message was communicated by Jesus?

God's Voice as Call

As is the case with any form of communication, people need to listen for God's voice in order to hear it. Even when we are listening, however, hearing God can be difficult. We live in a complex and noisy culture with loud messages screaming at us all the time—from roadside billboards, pop-up ads on our computers, radio broadcasts, movies, and television. God's voice is, by contrast, almost always quiet. God does not compete for our attention by trying to outyell everyone else; God speaks softly. At least, that is what the ancient Jewish prophet Elijah said, describing God's voice not as a whirlwind or an earthquake or a raging fire but as a whisper so quiet it was like the "sound of sheer silence" (1 Kings 19:12). It seems logical to conclude that if God speaks softly, perhaps we should too. If God does not rant at the world, neither should we.

Every time we hear God's voice, it is a gift and never a personal achievement, never a cause for pride. If the word we think we have heard from God prompts pride and arrogance, we either misheard what God was saying or we were listening to a voice other than God's.

When we truly hear God speak, God's voice typically comes to us as a call. God speaks, we listen, and we feel as if we have been summoned and addressed. God never speaks merely to convey information; instead, God's call changes us. When we respond, we usually do so because God's voice entices us. We follow God's call because the call itself gives us the confidence to respond. But sometimes God's call can be difficult, leading us toward a way of life that may cause us pain or sacrifice in the service of others. Regardless of the nature of our calling, God's voice will, if we heed it, give us the courage and endurance we need.

Have you ever felt a special call from God? Was it different from your usual spiritual experience? What does a call add to simply being a Christian? *A DEEP RESPONSIBILITY A PERSONAL WARM INNER GLOW*

Sensing God's leading gives us confidence, and that is a precious commodity in our world. It is important to remember, however, that confidence is not certainty. Certainty brooks no doubts and pays no attention when others express concern or dismay. Certainty forges ahead without restraint. But confidence, while steadfast and determined, is also humble and cautious. Christians are confident because we trust in God, but we are humble because we know the limits of our own abilities. Christians are cautious because it is risky when God calls us into unfamiliar places that are beyond our comfort zones. Lesslie Newbigin, the British theologian and longtime missionary in India, explains: "The confidence proper to a Christian is not the confidence of one who claims posses- sion of demonstrable and indubitable knowledge. It is the confidence of one who has heard and answered the call that comes from God."[1]

God often speaks through the people around us. We hear God in the nurture and advice of loving parents. We hear God in the comments of our friends. We hear God in churches where people worship to- gether and care for one another. We hear God in the needs of our neighbors. We hear God in great works of art and music. We hear God in the warm embrace of a spouse and in the snuffling sounds of our sleeping children. And we hear God in words of counsel and advice from mentors and peers. As God's word comes to us through these other people, it no doubt often needs to be interpreted. We weigh what we hear and strive to discern God's voice in the mix.

> How do you distinguish between being properly confident and overly certain? Is it ever helpful to challenge someone's certitude? Can we really be confident and humble at the same time?

There may be times when God speaks directly to us. That can happen, but it has been a relatively rare occurrence in the long stretch of Christian history. Even if we are convinced that God has spoken directly to us, it is wise to ask others to confirm what we think we have heard. Early in his life, Francis of Assisi heard the voice of God telling him to "build my church." Interpreting that literally, Francis began to re- build an old stone chapel, rock by rock, out in the countryside. Only later did he realize that God wanted him to rebuild the church spiritually as the people of God, and he then began the Franciscan movement. It is comforting to know that even a saint doesn't always hear God correctly the first time, but with time we can all discern God's call.

General Revelation

The entire world is full of God's communicative presence. The nineteenth-century Catholic poet Gerard Manley Hopkins described creation as literally "charged with the grandeur of God." Like static electricity, he said, God's presence in creation is ready at any moment to "flame out, like shining from shook foil."[2] In the language of traditional theology, this grandeur and shining—God's constant voice in the world—is called general revelation.

General revelation is knowledge about God that is available to everyone as part of ordinary human experience. It is what leads the great majority of the world's people to believe there is a God. In the United States, opinion polls indicate that belief in God has held steady at well over 90 percent for the last one hundred years, and it is unlikely that the figure will decline markedly in the years ahead. On the global level, at least three-quarters of the world's population believes there is a God.

Belief in God is not by itself a distinguishing mark of Christian faith. In fact, we Christians inherited our monotheistic vision of God from our Jewish forebears, and Muslims share a similarly singular vision of God. Many Jews and Muslims, as well as people from other faiths, express great love for God, engage in what they believe is the devout worship of God, and seek to discover and do God's will as much as they are able. Christians should be respectful of these practices even when we disagree over doctrines and beliefs.

The apostle Paul can serve as a model. When visiting Athens, he first acknowledged and praised the religious fervor of its residents. He then sought to enlarge and correct some of their views of God, but he did so partly by quoting their own religious authorities back to them. The famous comment that in God "we live and move and have our being" (Acts 17:28) is taken from an ancient pagan religious poet. Paul recognized that the Athenians already possessed some knowledge of God. Rather than denounce everything they believed, he based his proclamation of Christian faith on the foundation of their already existing faith in God.

♦♦♦

How can we balance evangelism with respect for others? Can we disagree about our most deeply held beliefs and still respect one another? How much do we need to know about other religions? What have you learned from people of other faiths?

♦♦♦

Following Paul's example, Christians who study other religions with care and diligence are likely to be both better informed and more gracious in interactions with non-Christian neighbors and friends. And at times, we will find ourselves *learning from*, not merely *learning about*, people of other faiths. This should not surprise us. In Jesus' story of the good Samaritan (Luke 10:25–37), the hero is a member of a heretical sect—a follower of a false religion. That same scenario occurs today: Sometimes people of other faiths act and think more Christianly than people who are followers of Jesus.

Throughout the history of Christianity, Christians have borrowed ideas from people of other faiths and have used those ideas to explain Christian faith to people who have never heard of Jesus. This is sometimes called apologetics, which means explaining why you hold certain beliefs. (It is not about apologizing for holding such views.) Christians engage in the work of apologetics because they believe faith is reasonable as well as true. Because faith is reasonable rather than irrational, it just might be possible to prove the existence of God without special appeal to either the Bible or Christian tradition. Many Christian philosophers have tried to do just that.

One of the greatest of these philosophers was Thomas Aquinas, who composed many proofs for the existence of God. His famous proof from causality goes like this: Everything that takes place in the world has a cause. This means that every cause itself must have some kind of prior cause. If we follow this series of causes and prior causes back far enough in time, we will ultimately come to the original cause that started everything else rolling. Aquinas called this original cause the "first cause," and he identified that first cause with God. He was convinced that on the basis of this kind of logic every human being could possess knowledge that God exists.[3]

These kinds of proofs have never convinced everyone—no philosophic argument can ever do that—but most Christians think general revelation provides enough evidence to make belief in God reasonable, even if the existence of God can never be absolutely proved. It is thus proper for Christians sometimes to argue with other people about their faith, as long as such arguing is civil and reasonable. Graciousness does not preclude debate. What graciousness requires is respect for the other person and a genuine willingness to listen to what another person is saying. If Christians would consistently model respectful debate with members of other faiths (and, for that matter, with other Christians with whom they disagree), they could become helpful exemplars of civil dialogue for a world in serious need of that skill.

What proofs of God's existence make the most sense to you? To what degree is Christianity rational, and to what degree must Christianity be taken on faith alone?

Jesus as God's Word

If everyone already has some knowledge of God, what is it that distinguishes a Christian view of God from others? What does Christianity add to the mix of what humanity has learned about God from reason and nature alone? For the Bible and most Christians, the crucial question has to do with God's character—*Who* is God?—and the classic Christian answer has always been that Jesus provides us with the purest and clearest glimpse of God's person and character we will ever have on earth.

Jesus was God incarnate, and everything he said and did reveals God to us. But what a strange revelation this was! When God came to earth, there were no trumpet blasts or accoutrements of power. God did not make a grand entrance like a king or a judge. God did not come demanding worship and honor. God did not come to make the earth shake and people quake. Instead, God came to earth as a little baby born to a young Jewish woman named Mary in a backwater region of the Roman Empire. God arrived in scaled-down size, accommodated to our needs and limited abilities, in a form that was fully human while also fully divine.

The way Jesus expressed himself was similarly unexpected. Instead of giving straightforward answers to straightforward questions, Jesus told stories, and he also offered his followers a variety of short, pithy, and sometimes paradoxical adages to guide them on their way. These parables and sayings are recorded in the four New Testament Gospels of Matthew, Mark, Luke, and John.

We can picture ourselves as characters in the stories Jesus told. A widow has lost a coin and will not rest until it is found. Laborers hired late in the afternoon are paid the same as those

♦ ♦

In which of Jesus' parables can you most easily see yourself? Which parable surprises you the most or makes you most uncomfortable?

♦ ♦

who worked all day, and the people who worked all day are upset. A traveler is accosted, and a total stranger—a person he would have shunned in any ordinary encounter—helps him. There are stories about weddings and deaths, about kings and paupers, about baking bread and discovering hidden treasures.

What is the point? Almost all of Jesus' parables require us to evaluate how we would respond in the same situations. They engulf us, turning the spotlight of inquiry on us. Jesus seems to be saying that knowledge of God cannot be held at arm's length. It is not controllable like other forms of knowledge. It knocks us off balance and makes us the object of scrutiny. Instead of putting God under the microscope, the parables of Jesus hold us up for examination.

The short sayings of Jesus have much the same effect. Jesus told his followers that the first will be last and the last will be first. He said that the meek will inherit the earth. He said that when someone strikes us on one cheek, we should offer our other cheek to be struck as well. He said the best way to gain your life is to lose it. And Jesus told his followers never to worry about what they are going to eat or what they are going to wear and never to judge another human being.

These sayings all reverse the normal order of the world. They turn things upside down. Instead of giving answers or information about God, they pose questions to us. And that is exactly the point. Jesus provides knowledge of God that can be known only in relationship, and the relationship that God offers is one that transforms us.

◆◆◆◆◆◆◆◆◆◆◆◆◆◆◆◆◆◆◆◆◆◆◆◆◆◆◆◆◆◆◆◆◆◆◆

Which sayings of Jesus seem the clearest? Which are hardest to understand? Which are the most upsetting to you?

◆◆◆◆◆◆◆◆◆◆◆◆◆◆◆◆◆◆◆◆◆◆◆◆◆◆◆◆◆◆◆◆◆◆◆

The transforming power of a relationship with Jesus is the thesis of every Christian testimony. The popular writer Frederica Mathewes-Green describes her own transformational encounter with Jesus in her book *At the Corner of East and Now*. She was on her honeymoon in Europe and, at the time, considered herself a Hindu. Then she came upon a marble statue of Christ in one of the niches on a side wall of a church, and this is what happened:

I was standing there looking at the statue, and then I discovered I was on my knees. I could hear an interior voice speaking to me. Not with my ears—it was more like a radio inside suddenly clicking on. The voice was both intimate and authoritative, and it filled me. It said, "I am your life. You think that your life is your name, your personality, your history. But that is not your life. I am your life." . . . I stood up feeling pretty shaky. It was like sitting quietly in your living room and having the roof blown off. . . . If someone had asked me a half hour earlier, I would have said I was not sure [Jesus] had ever lived. Yet here he was, and though I didn't know him, it seemed he already knew me, from the deepest inside out.[4]

What we learn about God through Jesus is like that. In Jesus, we see God as a person, not as an abstract spiritual power, and as a person who cares deeply about us. Instead of offering quantifiable information about God, Jesus provides relational knowledge of God that can never be fully translated into propositional form. None of this detracts from the factuality of Jesus' life, death, and resurrection. Nor does it minimize the need to think reasonably and logically about

◆◆◆◆◆◆◆◆◆◆◆◆◆◆◆◆◆◆◆◆◆◆◆◆◆◆◆◆◆◆◆◆◆◆◆

Have you ever experienced anything like what Frederica Mathewes-Green describes? Is everyone supposed to have this kind of dramatic religious experience? How might knowledge of God change us slowly?

◆◆◆◆◆◆◆◆◆◆◆◆◆◆◆◆◆◆◆◆◆◆◆◆◆◆◆◆◆◆◆◆◆◆◆

what we believe. But the knowledge of God that Christ provides goes deeper. It is living knowledge that invades our lives and changes us forever, moving us in the direction of becoming the kinds of people we were created to be and that, deep inside us, we truly want to be.

This kind of knowledge is humbling. Instead of inflating our pride, it deflates it. Knowledge of God is not something we can claim to have obtained by our own effort. It is not like getting an A in a class by means of our own hard work. It is not something we achieve by our own wits and skill.

Instead, it is a gift. God graciously helps us see reality more clearly, including the reality of who God is and who we are. It gives us confidence and compassion simultaneously. It weds knowledge to love and thus draws us closer to both God and our neighbors.

Prayer

Prayer is central to the Christian life. To be at prayer is to be willing to hear what God is saying and to be ready to respond appropriately. Long before it involves our saying anything, prayer is listening. It is attentiveness, being in the presence of God, waiting expectantly for God to speak to our hearts. Alluding to the story in the fourth chapter of John in which Jesus asks a Samaritan woman to give him a drink from a well, the *Catechism of the Catholic Church* says that the mystery of prayer is that Jesus "first seeks us and asks us for a drink. Jesus thirsts; his asking arises from the depths of God's desire for us. Whether we realize it or not, prayer is the encounter of God's thirst with ours. God thirsts that we may thirst for him."[5]

The ongoing, ceaseless thirst of prayer is not only about listening; it is also about speech. In prayer, we not only listen for God's voice but also speak: expressing wonder, voicing gratitude, verbalizing our worries, confessing our sins, asking for help. And well we should. Jesus said that God is deeply interested in each of us as persons—he said God knows the numbers of hairs on our heads—and prayer follows the personal contours of our lives. Our prayers reflect our joys and sorrows, our successes and failures, our hopes and fears.

In many ways, prayer is a mystery—everything we bring to God, God already knows—but we are commanded to pray nonetheless. Somehow our prayers flow together with God's own will to impact the world. At times, it is virtually impossible *not* to pray. We have to cry out to God for help, or to express gratitude for what we have received, or to confess our sins, or to praise the beauty of creation. If we stifle those prayers, we lose touch with our humanity. Put simply, prayer is integral to being human. It is part of our God-given nature and part of our natural and normal response to God and to the world.

But not all Christian prayers are natural, and the most unnatural of all is prayer for one's enemies. This is, however, a requirement Jesus has placed on us; it is part of the Jesus creed. Praying

How often do you pray? What do you pray for? When has prayer been most meaningful to you? Have you ever prayed for your enemies?

for our enemies goes against all our gut feelings about the world. Our natural inclination is to damn our enemies, imploring God to crush them on our behalf. But God is not our hired gun. In fact, God loves our enemies as much as us, and that makes everything much more complicated.

Jesus said that God makes the rain fall on the just and the unjust alike. God treats everyone fairly. God treats everyone mercifully. God loves everyone, and we are called to do the same. This is where prayer and ethics meet. We are not required merely to *act* nicely toward those we hate, forcing ourselves to be civil and polite; we are supposed to genuinely care for our enemies. Learning to pray for them is a necessary first step. Praying for our enemies changes us. It nudges us—in fact, it sometimes forcefully shoves us—into seeing the world in a new way, closer to the way God sees it.

Prayer can be difficult, and sometimes prayer can run dry. There are times when the universe goes silent and God's presence seems to evaporate. This can happen when a loved one dies, when a marriage falls apart, when we learn we are deathly sick, when a disaster strikes our community, or when evil seems to triumph in war, terror, and injustice. Emptiness and despair are part of the human experience, and Christians are not exempt. These times of suffering and silence are deeply unsettling, but enduring them can deepen our souls and bind us to our neighbors in ways otherwise impossible.

Because we have known the silence of God, Christians can feel compassion for everyone else who experiences that silence. We do not have any pat answers that can magically make things right; only God can end the silence. So Christians weep with those who weep. We pray with and for those who cannot pray for themselves, following the model of Jesus, who asked his disciples to pray with him and for him in the Garden of Gethsemane on the night of his arrest, when Jesus himself experienced God's awful silence.

In his recent book *God Has a Dream*, the South African church leader Desmond Tutu says, "Dear Child of God, I am sorry suffering is not optional. It seems to be part and parcel of the human condition, but suffering can either embitter or ennoble."[6] Suffering is a difficult passageway that can help us become truly gracious Christians. As Christians, we are thankful for every word we hear from God, but God's silence can also be a way of instructing and changing us. In moments of despair, we sometimes have to ask others to listen for God's voice on our behalf. God does not always speak to us directly, but God is always there.

As Christians, we sometimes act as if we are the only people to whom God speaks, but that is not the case. Every person has some knowledge of God, some ability to hear and respond to God's voice. Jesus Christ, the living Word of God, is the most important way God has ever spoken to the world. Yet there are many other ways in which

◆◆◆◆◆◆◆◆◆◆◆◆◆◆◆◆◆◆◆◆◆◆◆◆◆◆◆◆◆◆◆◆

Has there been a time in your life when God was silent? How did you cope with that experience? Was anyone especially important in helping you?

◆◆◆◆◆◆◆◆◆◆◆◆◆◆◆◆◆◆◆◆◆◆◆◆◆◆◆◆◆◆◆◆

God can and does speak. Gracious Christianity is based, at least in part, on this conviction: God is present in the world ahead of us, speaking all the time, and our task is to hear and follow together.

4

The Fullness of Salvation

In the book of Ephesians, the apostle Paul describes salvation as involving all the vast and wonderful ways God is redeeming everything that exists, restoring goodness and beauty to the entirety of creation. Salvation, as seen from this grand-scale perspective, includes healing everything that is wrong with the world, but it goes beyond that. The goal of salvation is to refashion the world so that it will eventually become what it was meant to be, to raise the existence of the universe to a level never seen before and never imagined possible (1:3–23).

But salvation is not only about God's plans for the universe as a whole. It is also about us. Salvation reaches down into the smallest crevices of the human heart. When God's saving love enters our lives, we are transformed. In the same way that salvation on the grand scale both restores what has been lost and adds something more, personal salvation heals our broken souls and lifts us into a new life of love for God, others, and the entire creation.

But how does salvation take place? Is it a process? Is it an event? Is our own effort somehow involved? What makes salvation possible? How does salvation change us and our relationships with others?

Personal Salvation

At its core, personal salvation is the process through which we internalize God's love for us so that we, in turn, can externalize that love to others. When we enter the path of salvation, we are taken up into God's great work of love and re-creation, and we are given the opportunity to become active agents in that process of reclaiming and reforming the world. Writing to the church at Corinth, Paul says, "God, who reconciled us to himself through Christ . . . has given us the ministry of reconciliation" (2 Cor. 5:18). Salvation restores our relationship with God and allows us to become partners with God in the work of reconciling the rest of creation with the Creator.

A person's experience of salvation is deeply personal. Somehow, in some way, we come to understand that God loves us. And somehow, in some way, we embrace that love. This is an intimate encounter, and no two people experience it in exactly the same way. For some it is emotionally overwhelming; for others it is not. For some the primary feeling is surrender, for others relief, for still others joy.

One thing is certain: Salvation does not come in a one-size-fits-all package that applies to everyone. Reconciliation is the common destination, but the roads we travel to get there can differ considerably. Jesus told many stories about what it means to be reconciled, stories of lost sheep and lost coins that were found, of buried treasure discovered in a field, of people being born again and starting their lives anew. As those multiple images of salvation imply, there is more than one way to experience God's grace and its impact on our lives.

Perhaps the most famous of Jesus' story-descriptions of salvation is the parable of the prodigal son (Luke 15:11–32).

This is a tale of a man who has two sons. The older child is thoroughly loyal and absolutely faithful—always there to help out, always responsible, and apparently always keeping track of just how much he has done for his father. The younger son is a free spirit who wants to get out from under his father's thumb as quickly as possible. So the younger son asks for his inheritance in advance, and his father finally acquiesces.

Money in hand, the young son goes off to live the good life, but soon his funds are gone and he is reduced to poverty. Destitute, he takes up work as a laborer on a farm and eventually even considers eating the garbage he is supposed to feed the pigs. Disgusted with himself and knowing that even the poorest member of his father's staff is better off than he, the young man goes home to see if his father will take him back, not as a son but merely as a servant.

So the prodigal makes his way home, hesitant, embarrassed, and stinky. And what does he find? A cold and distant father who tells him he is no longer welcome? A disgruntled father who tells him to eat with the pigs? An arrogant father who wants his son to grovel at his feet? No, he does not find anything like that. Instead, he finds a father who has hoped for his return every day since he left. A father who runs to his son and hugs him. A father who welcomes him back with the biggest party he has ever thrown. A father who simply loves him as his own dear child. But the older brother is incensed by this show of affection and refuses to come to the party. He is angry at both his father and his younger brother and sulks away.

This story illustrates both grace and ungraciousness, forgiveness and the failure to forgive, reconciliation and estrangement. The father bestows grace, the younger son accepts grace, and the older son is disgusted by the whole scene. The parable

Do you identify more with the older brother or the prodigal son? Is it easier to accept grace or extend grace? Can you think of a time when you observed a truly gracious act?

is about the nature of salvation—about the fact that God likes us as well as loves us. We are invited to accept God's grace in our lives in the same way that the prodigal son accepts his father's grace: thankfully, joyfully, and with the full knowledge that this is not what we deserve. It is a pure gift. Grace always is.

In the story of the prodigal son, salvation is dramatically depicted as a climactic moment when the father welcomes his son home. But that is not the only way grace can be experienced, not the only way salvation comes to us. Grace can also be gradually infused into our lives, working slowly and almost imperceptibly over extended periods of time, drawing us little by little into deeper fellowship with God and others. We see this alternative in the story Jesus told about a farmer scattering seeds (Luke 8:4–15). Some of the seeds fell on the path where people trampled them, some landed on rocks where they dried out and died before they could sprout, some germinated in places where they were choked by faster-growing weeds, and some landed in good soil where they grew, flowered, and eventually produced a crop of grain.

In explaining this parable, Jesus said the story is about how different people hear the Word of God and receive God's grace. Clearly, the last group in the parable represents the ideal. Of them the text says, "These are the ones who, when they hear the word, hold it fast in an honest and good heart, and bear fruit with patient endurance" (Luke 8:15). There is hardly any hint of drama in this description, no Jack-and-the-beanstalk miracle of sudden growth or miraculous transformation. It is all slow, steady, and gradual growth: first, the tiny sprout; then the emergence of roots; then the slow maturation of the plant; and finally, the production of flowers and seeds. None of this is rushed; it all takes time. Spiritually, some people are just like that. Grace grows slowly in their "honest and good hearts" and only slowly bears fruit as they wait "with patient endurance" for God's grace to mature in their lives.

This difference between slower and faster ways of experiencing grace is evident in individual biographies. Some people, following the model of the prodigal son, can point to a specific date and hour when they responded to God's saving grace. Others, following the seed parable, testify that God's work in their lives has been slow and gradual but persistent. This difference in personal experience is one of the factors that has encouraged the development of two patterns of baptism within the Christian church. Churches that assume that God's saving grace normally operates in a slow manner over long periods of time (such as the Catholic, Orthodox, and Lutheran churches) typically practice infant baptism and then nurture their young people gradually into faith. In Christian traditions that assume that God's normal mode of operating is more dramatic, dispensing saving grace at one identifiable moment (such as most Baptist and Pentecostal churches), individuals are usually baptized as adults after they testify to a decisive experience of conversion.

> ◆◆◆◆◆◆◆◆◆◆◆◆◆◆◆◆◆◆◆◆◆◆◆◆◆◆◆◆◆◆◆◆◆◆◆◆◆◆◆
>
> Are you more familiar with churches that emphasize fast grace or slow grace? What has been your own experience? What is your understanding of baptism?
>
> ◆◆◆◆◆◆◆◆◆◆◆◆◆◆◆◆◆◆◆◆◆◆◆◆◆◆◆◆◆◆◆◆◆◆◆◆◆◆◆

What Salvation Entails

The pace of grace in our lives is ultimately less significant than what grace does for us. What does salvation entail? Historically, Christians have said that salvation includes three dimensions: forgiveness, renewal, and reconciliation.

Forgiveness is required because we are sinful and imperfect creatures who harm one another frequently by our disdainful thoughts, unkind words, and uncaring actions. It is not just that we make mistakes—which, of course, we do—but that we choose to harm one another. Sometimes we do this in a premeditated way and at other times on the spur of the moment. Sometimes we do it directly, and sometimes it is indirect. Regardless of the details, this kind of behavior is sinful, and when we sin we incur guilt. We may not always feel ashamed of what we have done because our consciences can malfunction, but we are objectively guilty nonetheless.

In an obvious sense, we are guilty in relation to the people we have harmed, and we need their forgiveness. But we are also guilty in relation to God. Why? Because any intentional harm we do to others is a transgression of the law of love God has woven into creation, and it is also an affront to God's own continuing love for the world. Sin is sometimes defined as an offense against God's righteousness. This does not mean God takes offense because we break some arbitrary rule of religious etiquette. It means God wants what is right for the whole world, and our sins push the world in a different direction, away from God's righteousness toward evil and disorder.

◆ ◆

How effective do you think our consciences are in letting us know when we are guilty? How does feeling guilty compare with feeling ashamed?

◆ ◆

The remedy for guilt always involves confession: acknowledging the wrong we have done and taking responsibility for it. People can sometimes forgive us even when we have not confessed our wrongdoing, but we cannot experience that forgiveness unless we admit we need it. We cannot live at peace with others or ourselves if we are not honest about who we are and what we have done. And we cannot be at peace with God either. While confession can be painful and embarrassing, it is the only way forward.

Confession is required, but confession is not what forgives us. Forgiveness is a gift, and its source lies outside us. Forgiveness comes from someone else, and to be forgiven is a wonderful experience. Forgiveness itself, however, does not make us good; it only makes us forgiven. We will sin again, and we will need to be forgiven again. That is why the Protestant Reformer Martin Luther described the Christian life as one of ongoing repentance, a never-ending cycle of confession and forgiveness. This was the first of the famous Ninety-five

Theses that Luther nailed on the church door at Wittenburg in October 1517.

Renewal is the second aspect of salvation, and renewal does precisely what forgiveness cannot: It makes us better people. God's renewal of our lives makes us more fully alive and more genuinely good. If we picture ourselves like flat balloons all riddled with holes, forgiveness has the effect of patching up the holes, but it is the renewing power of God's Spirit that then fills us and helps us become the three-dimensional people we were meant to be. In the language of traditional theology, God's forgiveness of sins is called justification, while the renewal of our lives is called sanctification.

This renewal, or sanctification, of our lives takes time. It is a journey, and the goal is genuine holiness. Holiness refers to the fullness of life God intended for us from the beginning of creation, and it has both personal and social dimensions. God's renewal of our hearts and minds pushes us beyond our natural self-focus toward greater awareness of others. Walter Rauschenbusch, who is sometimes called the founder of the social gospel movement (a theological movement in the early twentieth century that stressed that sin and salvation have an impact on social structures as well as on individual lives), once said that salvation includes "the voluntary socializing of the soul."[1] True holiness makes us more attuned to the needs of others instead of focused on our own wants and desires.

We will never attain complete holiness in this lifetime. The final goal will always be ahead of us. But just as significantly, our progress in holiness can never be compared with anyone else's. We are not in spiritual competition with one another. We are not trying to outdo one another in a race around the bases toward perfection. God wants what is best for each of us, and the bases can be laid out in very different patterns. God has a special path for each of us, a special vocation we are called to fulfill, and we will find both holiness and personal meaning as we faithfully follow that path.

Finally, salvation includes *reconciliation*. The grand goal of salvation as articulated by Paul in the New Testament is the rec-

◆◆◆◆◆◆◆◆◆◆◆◆◆◆◆◆◆◆◆◆◆◆◆◆◆◆◆◆◆◆◆◆

Do you have a sense of vocation in your life?
What are the characteristics of that vocation?
How did you become aware of your vocation?
To what degree is reconciliation a part of your
Christian calling or vocation?

◆◆◆◆◆◆◆◆◆◆◆◆◆◆◆◆◆◆◆◆◆◆◆◆◆◆◆◆◆◆◆◆

onciliation of every part of creation with every other part and the reconciliation of the whole of creation with God, the Creator. Not only do we experience this reconciliation ourselves, but God also invites us to join in the ministry of reconciliation, participating in the huge and wonderful work of restoring creation.

The ministry of reconciliation includes evangelism, which breaks down barriers between God and humankind, and it also includes social action designed to break down the barriers of prejudice and injustice that drive people apart. It includes working for peace with people who are our obvious enemies, and it includes mending relationships on a daily basis with those we care about most. It involves learning how to love God better, and it involves loving the natural world too. All of this is included in the salvific work of reconciliation. Salvation is thus extended to all of life and is not limited to the spiritual dimension.

The grand work of reconciliation is, of course, not something we can do on our own. Reconciliation, like forgiveness and renewal, is a gift from God. It is God who will ultimately reconcile all things in heaven and earth in Christ. But God graciously invites us, despite our flaws and weaknesses, to be part of this great work. Salvation is personal, but it is also social and even cosmic, and the ultimate goal is for all of creation to participate in the mutuality of love that has always existed within the Trinity.

Jesus and Salvation

In the New Testament, Jesus stands at the center of the salvation story. It is Jesus who makes salvation possible. Yet it is the trinitarian God who loves us and saves us, not

Jesus alone. Sometimes sermons portray Christ as rescuing us from the unquenchable anger of God the Father, who would prefer to throw us into hell and torture us forever. But anything that implies a Father-versus-Son tug-of-war within the Trinity is misleading. It is the whole God who saves us—Father, Son, and Holy Spirit—and it is the whole God who loves and forgives us.

Jesus was the incarnation of God on earth for the sake of our salvation, and it is the entirety of his life, teachings, death, and resurrection that saves us. We are, in some sense, saved by Christ's birth and life among us. We are, in some sense, saved by Christ's teaching and example. We are also somehow saved by Christ's death and somehow saved by his resurrection. Salvation is ultimately a mystery,

♦ ♦

What is your primary image of God the Father? What is your image of Jesus? Do these images blend easily together, or is there tension between them?

♦ ♦

but we know that Jesus is at the center of salvation and that everything he said and did plays a part.

The mere fact of incarnation, that Jesus was willing to be born and live among us, is an important element of salvation. Like a famous guest who honors us by staying at our home or eating a meal with our family, God, in his presence on earth in the person of Jesus, honored the creation and, most specially, honored us as human beings.

Jesus became one of us. According to Athanasius, bishop of Alexandria in Egypt during the fourth century, Jesus somehow sanctified whatever he "assumed" (accepted into his own being) in the incarnation. What precisely this means is difficult to explain, in the same way that it is difficult to explain exactly why we feel honored when an important person visits us. Yet somehow the incarnation reassures us that it is good to be human. It tells us we do not need to be ashamed of being human, and we do not need to be saved from being human. God's presence with us in the baby Jesus and throughout his entire life on earth is a reaffirmation of God's original declaration of human goodness. In the same way that we become more beautiful when someone sincerely tells us we are beautiful, the incarnation is God's way of reminding us that we are good, and that reminder in some sense truly does make us better.

The life and teachings of Jesus also contribute to our salvation. Unlike Jesus, the rest of us are flawed and sinful—everyone of us—every parent, friend, mentor, spouse, and neighbor. So where do any of us find a model that demonstrates a better way? Where do we find an exemplar who can show us how we ought to live? The Christian answer is that we find that model in Jesus.

Several years ago, it was popular for young Christians to wear bracelets emblazened with the letters WWJD: What Would Jesus Do? That is a good question to ask in any situation. While we face circumstances far different from those in first-century Palestine, the basic human issues—our relationship with God, our relationships with others, and our personal character—remain the same. The life of Jesus offers a pattern for dealing with those issues today. Christ's moral and spiritual example is itself part of the salvation God offers in Christ.

Salvation is about right living, but it is also about our inner selves, what Christians often refer to as the heart or the soul. The heart is the realm of the emotional. It is the part of us that can sometimes bring us to our knees in anguish and, at other times, practically lift us off the ground with joy. When our hearts are joyful, we feel truly alive; when our hearts are heavy, we feel like we are stumbling toward despair or even death. The heart is the core of our being, and it needs to be transformed in salvation. More than anything else, it is the cross that does this.

On the cross, Christ somehow took all our pain and hurt, as well as all the enormous amounts of sin and evil in the world, upon himself. We have been forgiven through that act, but, just as importantly, we can be emotionally and spiritually healed by

Christ's death. Jesus died on the cross for us in order that we might live. Christ suffered for us in order that we might be made whole. The cross is God's costly offer of grace that speaks to our hearts as much as to our heads. Salvation is holistic. It transforms the center of our being in ways that our minds can sometimes only dimly understand,

♦ ♦

What dimension of Christ's life, teachings, death, and resurrection is most meaningful to you? Has this changed as you have moved through various stages of life?

♦ ♦

restructuring the affective perceptions we have of ourselves, God, and the world and clearing the way for restored fellowship.

One can still validly ask, however, "Why the cross? Why the need for Christ's death?" In response, Christians have often used an analogy taken from the realm of law, explaining that Christ was our substitute on the cross and received the punishment we deserve for our sins. That analogy can be helpful, but the real meaning of the cross is about love, not law. It is God's miraculous way of breaking the power of everything that controls us, of clearing the paths that were blocked, drawing us back into fellowship with God and all of creation. The cross renews our hearts in a way that is impossible to put into words. It is much better experienced than explained.

The resurrection of Jesus from the dead is the final aspect of Christ's life that provides salvation. The resurrection is God's sign to the world that Jesus really was God's representative on earth. The resurrection validates everything that Jesus said and did, giving us confidence to trust his words and work. The resurrection also demonstrates God's power over the forces of evil, sin, and death. Christ's violent death was not the end of the story; killing Jesus did not get rid of him. The resurrection is a sign that righteousness is stronger than evil and that life will ultimately conquer death. Thus, for us, as for Jesus, the grave is not the end. By God's grace, we are part of a kingdom that is endless, the kingdom of God's boundless love. We do not know precisely what resurrection means—Jesus' resurrected body was not simply his revivified corpse; it was a different "glorified" body—but because of his resurrection, we possess the hope that one day we too will be united with God in a glorified body for all eternity.

This hope is described by the pastor, theologian, and psychological counselor Henri Nouwen as stretching "far beyond the limits of one's own psychological strength." Christian hope is not mere optimism but a new evaluation of the nature of reality based on "the historic Christ-event which is understood as a definitive breach in the deterministic chain of human trial and error, and as a dramatic affirmation that there is light on the other side of darkness."[2] The resurrection frees us from the fear of death and opens us to the love of others. Christian hope does not make us immune to pain and suffering, and it certainly does not mean that life will always be happy. But because we know that God's love for us transcends death, we can rest in God.

The power evident in the resurrection can be accessed in the present. This power is not, first of all, the power to work miracles, though it might include that. Instead, it is the power to love. It is love that drove Christ to the cross and love that raised Christ from the dead, and that love, when it finds a home in our own hearts, makes it possible for us to reflect God's love to others. A recent book by two Indian Catholic scholars describes the salvation made possible by the resurrection: "Jesus' victory over sin and death is . . . experienced in every act of love for the poor, the marginalized, the enemy, love of those from whom we expect no reward. Jesus' victory is present in every fight for justice which is impregnated with love, in every act of courage to protest when human beings are trampled upon . . . in every act of hope that God's reign will prevail in spite of the power of evil around us."[3] Just as it provides hope for the future, the resurrection provides courage and power to live in harmony with God's love in the present.

Salvation is both deeply personal and thoroughly social, and these two dimensions of salvation can never be separated. In the same way that the Jesus creed indissolubly links the love of God with the love of others, our personal salvation necessarily connects us more deeply with others. Rather than rescuing us out of the world, salvation redirects us back to the world as agents of God's goodness and grace.

5

The Spirit and Life

God's gracious love for the entire world is nowhere more evident than in the Holy Spirit. The Spirit blows through the world as the Spirit pleases without any Christian or churchly limitations. In one of the most famous conversations in the Bible, Jesus tells Nicodemus that, while the effects of the Spirit can be observed, no one ever knows where the Spirit is coming from or where it is going (John 3:8). In a sense, the Spirit is God for everyone.

At the famous Azusa Street Revival of 1906, where the modern Pentecostal movement was born, the work of the Spirit upset the social mores of the day when Africans, Europeans, Hispanics, and Asians all crowded together at the front of the church, praying for one another and seeking the Holy Spirit. Visitors were often shocked by this indiscriminate mixing of people across the lines of race, but the leaders of the revival saw it as a restoration of the multicultural fellowship of faith that the Holy Spirit had inaugurated long ago on the original day of Pentecost (Acts 2:1–21).

How are we to understand the surprising and embracing impact of the Holy Spirit? While the Spirit of God remains free and unpredictable, are there any generalizations we can make about the Spirit's work? What does the Spirit have to do with gracious Christianity?

The Spirit of Life

The Holy Spirit plays many roles in the world, but there is no doubt which is most fundamental: The Spirit is the source of life in all its wonderfully varied and diverse forms. The Nicene Creed, written in the fourth century, aptly and succinctly describes the Spirit as "the Lord, the Giver of Life." That is creedal rhetoric but also religious poetry. The Spirit of God is the Spirit of life, so the pleasure of existence is itself a gift from God. Indeed, the Spirit is the source of every aspect of who we are: physical, intellectual, psychological, and emotional. Nothing that is part of being human is divorced from the Spirit.

This life-giving role of the Spirit is vividly portrayed in the biblical story of Adam and Eve when God, having fashioned the first human body out of the dust of the ground, breathes the breath/spirit of life into that dusty figure and it comes alive (Gen. 2:7). In the book of Ezekiel (chap. 37), we see a similar effect as the scattered bones in a dry valley come rattling back to life as the Spirit blows over them. The book of Job (chap. 34) stresses the life-giving powers of the Spirit by saying that "all flesh would perish together, and all mortals return to dust" if God should ever "take back his spirit to himself, and gather to himself his breath" (vv. 14–15).

> When have you been most aware of the presence of the Holy Spirit in your life? Have there been times when the influence of the Spirit has seemed especially evident in your church, community, or world events?

The life-giving work of the Spirit applies not just to humanity but to all creation. If there is life, the Spirit is there. Because the Spirit is everywhere, the famous naturalist John Muir believed that the lowliest lichen on a rock possesses life from God in the same way as the tallest sequoia, the most beautiful elk, or the most intelligent human being. Every living thing possesses at least a tiny puff of God's enlivening breath; all life is sacred. Muir's views came close to pantheism, the belief that the world itself is divine. The world is not divine, and it is not to be worshiped, but life in all its many forms is indeed sacred in the sense that life comes from God.

It seems equally valid to say that the entire world belongs to God. Thus, no person or company or nation can really own the forests or the seas, and, most certainly, no one owns the air or the sun. A person may feel in partial control of a small bit of creation during the short span of a human life, but inevitably, even that will pass to others. We are merely sojourners on this planet, people who have the wonderful opportunity to enjoy the world while we are alive, to share it with others, and to leave it when we die in good shape—better, if possible—for those who come after us.

The role God assigned humanity in relation to nature is that of stewards and caretakers, and our caretaking needs to be truly care-full. Our role is not to force the natural world to serve our desires, and it is certainly not to destroy species or ecosystems at will. Instead, we are called to join with the Spirit in helping the natural world flourish. This responsibility should not be overly simplified or sentimentalized. Nature is complex and often cruel, and human intervention may sometimes be required. But intervention never means running roughshod over the world. Rather, we are called to nurture and protect the world as if it were a precious possession entrusted to us by our dearest friend with the stipulation that the earth's treasures be used for the benefit of all.

Out of respect for both creation and the Creator, many Christians throughout history have felt called to simplicity in living. We live in a culture that tells us happiness is found in owning things and that the more we own the happier we will be. But instead of deepening our lives or increasing our joy, the rush to accumulate possessions can make us shallow, greedy, and unsatisfied.

Living simply releases us from the tyranny of possessions and helps us appreciate the gift of life itself. It also redirects attention away from the newest fads and gadgets toward the basic necessities of life—food, water, shelter, and clothing—which so many people lack. Living simply on a voluntary basis is a discipline that brings to mind the millions of people who live simply, in poverty and on the brink of starvation, because they have no other choice. The Bible repeatedly identifies two groups of people who often need special assistance: widows and orphans. Today, single women with children (whether they are widows or find themselves on their own for some other reason) are often the most vulnerable members of society. Simplicity in living helps us to remember the needs of everyone who is vulnerable and whose grip on life may be precarious.

◆◆◆◆◆◆◆◆◆◆◆◆◆◆◆◆◆◆◆◆◆◆◆◆◆◆◆◆◆◆◆◆◆◆

What does it mean to be a steward of creation? What is our responsibility to the natural world? Should all Christians live simply, or is living simply a special calling meant only for some?

◆◆◆◆◆◆◆◆◆◆◆◆◆◆◆◆◆◆◆◆◆◆◆◆◆◆◆◆◆◆◆◆◆◆

Yielding to the Spirit

The Holy Spirit comes to make us more human, more fully alive, and more energetic. The Spirit makes us more aware of all the truth, goodness, and beauty that exists in the world. And the Spirit also makes us more sensitive to those situations in which life is currently being diminished by oppression, injustice, or prejudice. Where life is full, the Spirit inspires us to celebrate that fullness; where life is threatened or oppressed, the Spirit calls forth compassion and gives us the power to endure pain and to seek change. People who yield to the Spirit's leading rejoice with those who rejoice, weep with those who weep, and work for change wherever life is under siege.

Some people equate the notion of yielding to the Spirit with simple passivity. They seem to assume that being led by the Spirit necessarily involves less of their own initiative—less thinking, less deciding, less enjoying, less exerting themselves to get things done, and less risk taking. This view presupposes that the relationship between our own activity and the Spirit's work is a zero-sum game in

♦♦♦♦♦♦♦♦♦♦♦♦♦♦♦♦♦♦♦♦♦♦♦♦♦♦♦♦♦♦♦♦♦♦♦

How are our own thinking processes related to the guidance of the Holy Spirit? How does our work and effort relate to the influence of the Spirit in the world?

♦♦♦♦♦♦♦♦♦♦♦♦♦♦♦♦♦♦♦♦♦♦♦♦♦♦♦♦♦♦♦♦♦

which the only way to have more of one is to have less of the other. But the Holy Spirit comes to enhance our humanity, not to diminish it. Of course, some people identify the work of the Spirit too easily with their own wholly human impulses and intuitions. While the Spirit enhances life, the Spirit does not sanction everything we want to do. Yielding to the Spirit does involve putting some limits on our wants and desires.

The Spirit's ultimate goal, however, is positive: to give people what the Gospel of John calls eternal life (see John 3:16 and 17:3 for examples). The Greek term for "eternal" means both the quantitative notion of life without end and the qualitative notion of life lived on a higher plane. To have eternal life is in some small measure to have the same kind of life that God has. It is life that is full and rich and passionate and joyful. It is a quality of life that foreshadows what we will experience fully and forever with God and all the saints in heaven.

Spiritual Maturity

Fullness of life in the Spirit is a gift from God. We cannot claim it by our own strength nor manufacture it by our own effort. Yet our capacity to experience it can be enlarged when we allow the Holy Spirit to lead us forward into life. If we are willing, the Spirit will take on a role in our lives akin to a personal trainer, guiding us toward maturity through a process of discipline and exercise.

Spiritual training, like physical training, requires exercise. Gerald Sittser, author of *The Will of God as a Way of Life*, says that the main path to spiritual maturity—the main set of exercises the Spirit wants us to do every day—is, not surprisingly, to love God with our entire being and to love our neighbors as ourselves. He says that practicing these "basic responsibilities" of the Christian life is like practicing "the fundamentals of dribbling, passing, and shooting" in basketball.[1] In other words, the Jesus creed provides Christians with the basic drill instructions, and our responsibility is to practice them daily.

In helping us follow the path laid out by Jesus, the Holy Spirit often guides and encourages us in fairly mundane ways: through strangers who give us the opportunity to treat them as neighbors, through friends who allow us to rejoice with them when something good has happened, through the words of a newspaper article or television program reminding us of responsibilities toward those in poverty, through traffic jams that test our patience, through unexpected kindnesses that give us opportunities to say thanks. By training us through our daily routines, the Spirit prepares us to respond graciously when we encounter new situations that push us outside our zones of comfort.

◆◆◆◆◆◆◆◆◆◆◆◆◆◆◆◆◆◆◆◆◆◆◆◆◆◆◆◆◆◆◆◆◆◆

Who is the most spiritually mature person you know? What seems to motivate that person? How much or little is that person concerned with being perceived as deeply spiritual?

◆◆◆◆◆◆◆◆◆◆◆◆◆◆◆◆◆◆◆◆◆◆◆◆◆◆◆◆◆◆◆◆◆◆

There are no secret marks of maturity in Christian faith. Everything is up front and out in the open. As described by Paul, Christian maturity is measured by the degree to which our lives reflect the fruit of the Spirit, which consists of "love, joy, peace, patience, kindness, generosity, faithfulness, gentleness, and self-control" (Gal. 5:22–23). Christian maturity is a function of the way we live and the attitudes we exhibit. If we pray all day but treat others with disdain, our prayers are meaningless. If we study the Bible all the time but do not genuinely love our neighbors, our study is for naught. If we profess great love for God but never lift a finger to help others, our supposed love for God is hollow. The famous Orthodox collection of writings on spirituality called the *Philokalia* warns against putting even prayer ahead of concern for one's neighbor. It says, "Visit the sick, console the distressed, and do not make your longing for prayer a pretext for turning away from anyone who asks for your help; for love is greater than prayer."[2]

A similar point is made by Jesus in the story he told about the final judgment when God is portrayed as a shepherd sorting out the "sheep," who have done God's will on earth, from the "goats," who have not (Matt. 25:31–46). In this parable, the sheep are defined as those who have given food to the hungry, water to the thirsty, clothing to the naked, and shelter to the homeless and who have visited people who were sick or in prison. The sheep are rewarded with heaven. The goats have done none of these things, and they are told to depart from God's presence. Once again, spiritual maturity is equated with actions on behalf of others rather than with personal piety. It is also interesting that the sheep seem unaware of having done anything particularly good or spiritual. It appears that living in the Spirit is often a matter of unself-consciously caring for others, helping to preserve life when it is threatened, and reinvigorating life when it is beaten down.

The Bible also speaks of more dramatic gifts of the Holy Spirit that are given to specific individuals. These include special abilities such as teaching, preaching, healing, prophesying, the

Does every Christian have a special spiritual gift or gifts? Do gifts differ from talents? Can spiritual gifts be abused? What happens if they are ignored?

discernment of spirits, and speaking in tongues (see Rom. 12:6–8; 1 Cor. 12:7–11). These special gifts of the Spirit are to be celebrated and treasured for what they are, but they should not be seen as in any way trumping the more ordinary working of the Spirit. They are intended to extend and deepen the ordinary work of the Spirit in our lives. While they are given to individuals, they are not intended for individualistic use. Instead, the gifts of the Spirit are to build up the entire body of believers and to benefit all people. In fact, it may be more accurate to describe these spiritual gifts as gifts given to the world *through* a person rather than as gifts specifically given *to* a person. The gifts of the Spirit always serve the goals of the Spirit, and the Spirit's desire is to help everyone become better lovers of God, better lovers of other people, and better caretakers of the created order.

The Cost and Joy of Discipleship

In ordinary life, saying yes to one thing often means saying no to something else, and life in the Spirit is no exception. Saying yes to life in the Spirit will sometimes require saying no to certain desires, impulses, familiar routines, or old habits that are a part of our lives.

Saying yes or no is the way life works. When we go to a restaurant and pick one meal from the menu, it means we are not picking all the other items that are available. When we choose to attend one college or accept one job offer, we say no to all the others. When we marry one person, we leave all other suitors behind. Every accomplished musician, athlete, doctor, and artist has spent hours and hours practicing skills and honing them to perfection, and all of that practice has involved saying no to many other pleasant pursuits. In a similar manner, saying yes to the Spirit means saying no to a variety of other ways of living in the world.

Saying yes or no to the Spirit is, of course, also saying yes or no to Jesus, and that choice is often portrayed as a decision between life and death. In fact, Christians say that being a follower of Jesus in some way requires our own deaths. The German theologian Dietrich Bonhoeffer put it bluntly: "When Christ calls a man, he bids him come and die."[3]

Bonhoeffer knew something about how weighty choices can be. When Hitler came to power, Bonhoeffer had the opportunity to leave Germany, but he ultimately decided to stay home and help his fellow Christians respond to the evils of Nazism. A leader of the Christian resistance movement known as the Confessing Church, Bonhoeffer was eventually arrested and put to death for his involvement in an assassination plot against Hitler.

Bonhoeffer's choices led to his physical death, but his theological writings spoke of a different kind of dying: Following Jesus requires the death of our self-will. The human will, deformed by sin, is selfish and small and addicted to comfort and ease. We place our desires ahead of the desires and even the genuine needs of others. But if we truly want to be a Christian, said Bonhoeffer, such self-centeredness has to die. He used language that was stark: To be a Christian is to be crucified with Christ. As long as we hold on to our own comforts and place ourselves ahead of others, we are not loving others with the self-giving love that God displays toward us. Saying no to our self-centeredness accompanies saying yes to God's gracious love for us and all people.

> Do contemporary North Americans ever face literal death because of saying yes to Jesus? Does saying yes to God always involve a risk of some kind?

Bonhoeffer described a second death that is required of Christians, the death of vengeance and revenge. He likened this death to the death of Christ on the cross, saying that "as Christ bears our burdens, so we ought to bear the burdens of our fellow-men." The burden Christ bore on the cross, and the hardest burden any of us will ever have to bear, is the burden of forgiving the sins of others. In his typically straightforward prose, Bonhoeffer wrote, "Forgiveness is the Christlike suffering which it is the Christian's duty to bear."[4] Saying yes to God's forgiveness of us requires that we also forgive others; the two are inseparable.

Bonhoeffer believed that the end result of this dying to self and dying for others was not what might be expected. Instead of producing gloom or dreariness, the result was "ever increasing joy in the Lord."[5] Saying no to those things that hinder our relationship with God and that undermine our relationships with others does not diminish us; it enlarges us so we can more fully respond to God's offer of life and can share that life with others. Only through dying to self can we truly live. Only by forgiving others can we experience the joy of our own full forgiveness.

In the long history of Christianity, perhaps no one has represented the joy of costly discipleship better than Francis of Assisi. Francis lived in the thirteenth century, and his contemporaries called him God's court jester. He exuded love for God and all living things; he personified joy. But Francis was also known for his self-effacing service to others, especially for his love of lepers, the most reviled social outcasts of his day. He had grown up rich but had left his family's wealth behind to become voluntarily poor so that possessions would never interfere with his love for God or his service to others. He so identified with the pain of Jesus that later in life Francis developed what are called the stigmata, bleeding wounds on the hands, feet, and side that parallel the wounds of Christ on the cross.

Do you know anyone like St. Francis? What might it mean to be an instrument for peace in your local situation or in the world? Is it ever appropriate to place one's own needs ahead of the needs of others?

Francis understood the full depth and breadth of the human experience, and because of that he understood the full range of the Spirit's work in the human world. His vision of discipleship was accordingly deep and rich and passionate and life affirming, as captured in the famous prayer that is attributed to him:

> Lord, make me an instrument of your peace.
> Where there is hatred let me sow love,
> Where there is injury let me sow pardon,
> Where there is doubt, faith,
> Where there is despair, hope,
> Where there is darkness, light,
> Where there is sadness, joy.
> O Divine Master,
> Grant that I may not seek so much to be consoled as to
>   console,
> To be understood as to understand,
> To be loved as to love.
> For it is in giving that we receive,
> It is in forgiving that we are forgiven,
> And it is in dying that we are born to eternal life.[6]

Perhaps better than any other statement outside the Bible, the prayer of St. Francis lays out the pathway to gracious Christianity. It describes the way of life to which the Holy Spirit calls us and the life for which the Holy Spirit gives us power and strength.

6

Being Church

Church is the group name for being Christian. It refers to all the followers of Jesus who have ever lived. This includes people who are Catholic and Protestant, Eastern Orthodox and Amish, Lutheran and Methodist, Pentecostal and Baptist, and it includes many people who are not part of any organized denomination at all. This is the church in its largest scope.

More intimately, and just as importantly, church refers to a local gathering of believers, people who know one another face-to-face, people who put up with one another's quirks and foibles, people who genuinely try to love one another despite all their imperfections. The local community of the church is the social context in which Christianity takes living form. Being church is being Christian together.

What distinguishes the church from other organizations that bring people together? What is it that defines the church as church? What is the relationship of the church to the rest of the world? What is the relationship of the church to the kingdom of God as Jesus preached it?

The Church as Community

Cyprian, the third-century bishop of Carthage in North Africa, once famously set forth the proposition that there is no salvation outside the church. Even if that is an overstatement, he had a point. From the earliest days of Christianity, fellowship with other followers of Jesus—visible fellowship, physical fellowship, fellowship that acknowledges our total humanity—has been a necessary part of being Christian.

There are many New Testament images of the church, but virtually all of them stress relationships. Christians are called the people of God, citizens of a new city, guests invited to a wedding, the body of Christ. Freelance Christianity is seen as an anomaly. In the early centuries of the Christian movement, a person was considered merely a seeker—not a full Christian—until publicly baptized and welcomed visibly into the community of the church. A commitment to the church was seen as a necessary qualification for being a Christian. Christians belong to a household of faith and are not individual entrepreneurs for God.

The church as community does not require conformity. Christians are not meant to be cookie-cutter copies of one another. The naturally grumpy have a place in the community of the church along with the constitutionally cheery. Every other kind of personality has a place too: people who are spontaneous and people who plan everything in advance; people who are argumentative and people who try to smooth over all disagreements; people who like contemporary music and people who prefer classical; people who are intellectual and those who are not.

The community of the church is characterized by unity, not unanimity—by our mutual concern for one another, not by our becoming mirror images of one another. We look out for one another. We help one another when help is needed. We make sure no one is left behind as we move ahead. We rejoice with those who are celebrating, and we weep with those who are experiencing loss, grief, and pain. We bear one another's burdens. We use our gifts and talents for the good of all. Just as crucially, we acknowledge how much we ourselves need to be recipients of the help, care, love, and compassion of others.

There is perhaps no better symbol of this mutuality within the Christian community than the practice of foot washing. This ancient ritual of having one's feet washed and washing another's—a ritual that is all too rare in the contemporary church—physically demonstrates our acceptance of one another and wordlessly acknowledges our own neediness.

♦♦♦♦♦♦♦♦♦♦♦♦♦♦♦♦♦♦♦♦♦♦♦♦♦♦♦♦♦♦♦

What has been your experience of church? Is your church characterized by mutual concern? How have you helped others in your church? How have you been helped? How does your church differentiate between unity and unanimity?

♦♦♦♦♦♦♦♦♦♦♦♦♦♦♦♦♦♦♦♦♦♦♦♦♦♦♦♦♦♦♦

The Church for Others

The church is the place where the story of our personal redemption branches out and intertwines with the stories of other persons seeking redemption on the road toward full salvation. That road cannot be traveled alone. We need to traverse it in a caravan in which we can all share what the writer Anne Lamott calls the "rusty bent old tools [of] friendship, prayer, conscience, and honesty" to keep our wagons of faith rolling along.[1]

When the church practices this kind of mutual hospitality within its ranks, the result is a natural overflowing of hospitality to others. Genuine hospitality is hard to constrain within the boundaries of one's own community. Hospitable Christians will thus find themselves welcoming others into their midst and forgiving others as well. By contrast, whenever we try to limit our love and concern to those inside the church, those virtues tend to dry up at the spring. The purpose of Christian love is to serve the entire world, not to feather our own already cozy nests of faith to make them more comfortable.

This overflowing love is exemplified in acts both large and small. It is evident in the way church members in the little village of Le Chambon in southern France helped hide their Jewish neighbors when the Nazis took over the town during World War II. Eventually, their actions were discovered, and the pastor and other parishioners were arrested. When asked why they risked themselves in this way, they replied that they simply had no other option if they wanted to call themselves Christian. It was what their faith required.[2]

A similar sense of empathy and compassion is evident in less dramatic fashion whenever churches run soup kitchens to feed the hungry, programs to aid single mothers, shelters for the homeless, after-school activities for latchkey kids, halfway homes for people just out of prison, rehab programs for drug addicts, and local health clinics. Because every person is worthy of love, churches reach beyond their congregations to help those around them. And Christians often reach out to the world more broadly, contributing to international aid, famine and disaster relief, medical assistance, educational institutions, and economic development programs.

◆◆◆◆◆◆◆◆◆◆◆◆◆◆◆◆◆◆◆◆◆◆◆◆◆◆◆◆◆◆◆◆

In what ways does your church display compassion beyond its membership? Are there ministries of compassion your church might develop? In what such ministries are you or might you want to be involved? Since a church cannot give equal attention to every problem in society, how does your church determine its priorities?

◆◆◆◆◆◆◆◆◆◆◆◆◆◆◆◆◆◆◆◆◆◆◆◆◆◆◆◆◆◆◆◆

True compassion is neither blind nor stupid. Hospitable people know that sometimes people will take advantage of them, but they open their arms anyway because they know how much they themselves have received from God and others. The result is self-sustaining. The church becomes a school of mutual hospitality where the opening and reopening of our lives to one another in welcome, forgiveness, repentance, and hope slowly mold us into people of true and genuine compassion.

The Church and the Kingdom of God

The church is composed of people who understand what God is doing in the world or who have, at least, a hazy glimpse of it. The church is not, of course, the only conduit God has for getting things done in the world. God can work outside the church. What makes the church unique, however, is that its members know something about God's grand plan for the world, and they actively seek to cooperate with that plan.

The goal of the church is to help establish the kingdom of God on earth. The kingdom of God was a key theme in much of Jesus' preaching and teaching. That kingdom—which is better translated as the reign of God or the rule of God—exists wherever and whenever God's will is being done, regardless of who is doing it and whether or not it is done with self-conscious awareness.

Unlike the church, the kingdom of God is not something to which a person *belongs*; instead, it is something in which one *participates* to a greater or lesser extent. Whenever justice is honestly sought, or mercy is genuinely offered, or love is truly evident, the kingdom of God is present in some way and to some degree. Jesus described the kingdom in his famous Sermon on the Mount (Matt. 5–7). It is a way of living in which people trust God, serve others, judge no one, pray for enemies, and refuse to retaliate. It is a way of being human that is welcoming and inclusive.

From the very beginning, the church worked to establish the kingdom of God by extending charity to those in need. In the second century, the church in Rome provided free meals for hundreds of people every day, even though the church was still illegal and faced persecution. Across the centuries and around the globe, the church has frequently exerted a positive influence. Schools have been started, hospitals have been built, the cruelty of rulers has been mitigated, and aid has been given to those who are suffering. Christians have a well-documented history of generosity and compassion.

But while Christians have done much good, a realistic appraisal of the church's record is full of cautionary tales. Paul once said that Christians possess the treasure of the gospel in jars of clay (2 Cor. 4:7). Clay jars are flawed and fragile and easily broken, regardless of what they con-

◆◆

What is the church's current reputation in the world? Are Christians more well known for doing good or harm? Regardless of whether that reputation is deserved, what can be done to improve it?

◆◆

tain. The church has been entrusted with precious treasure, but sometimes its flaws are very visible.

Perhaps the saddest and most damning example is the church's historic treatment of Jews. The history of anti-Semitism—replete with murder, torture, rape, persecution, and forced migration—is largely a history of Christian anti-Judaism. Sadly, this anti-Judaism has not been peripheral to the Christian movement, and some of the most well-known and beloved saints of Christian history have been involved.

Another example of the church's failure is Christian complicity in the African slave trade from the 1600s through the 1800s. The ex-slave and abolitionist Frederick Douglass once contrasted the false faith of slave-making Christianity with the genuine Christianity of Christ, saying that the difference between the two was so large that "to be the friend of one, is of necessity to be the enemy of the other." Douglass declared shortly before the Civil War, "I love the pure, peaceable, and impartial Christianity of Christ: I therefore hate the corrupt, slaveholding, women-whipping, cradle-plundering, partial and hypocritical Christianity of this land."[3]

The list of Christian failures is shameful and long, including the many times Christians have killed and mistreated other Christians. Christians sometimes speak glibly about their love for one another, but global realities from Northern Ireland to the Balkans to Rwanda paint a different picture. Noting how frequently Christians are at war with one another, one Christian leader has suggested that a modest first step toward global peace would be for Christians to agree not to kill one another.

Long ago the Hebrew prophet Micah wrote that God requires three things of every person: "to do justice, and to love kindness, and to walk humbly with your God" (6:8). Christians have sometimes equated their own human hopes and desires with the kingdom of God, presuming that God must surely share their values and views. But whenever we assume that God is thoroughly and absolutely on our side, justice can easily be pushed aside, kindness can dissipate, humility can be forgotten, and the church can lose touch with the kingdom it exists to serve. The one sure way to avoid that catastrophe is to remember Micah's advice.

♦♦♦♦♦♦♦♦♦♦♦♦♦♦♦♦♦♦♦♦♦♦♦♦♦♦♦♦♦♦♦♦♦♦

Is there a tension between justice and kindness? Are both justice and kindness required of peacemakers? How is humility related to the task of working for peace and justice?

♦♦♦♦♦♦♦♦♦♦♦♦♦♦♦♦♦♦♦♦♦♦♦♦♦♦♦♦♦♦♦♦♦♦

The Church and the State

Merely by existing, the church declares God's presence in the world. Because the church takes its cues from God, as opposed to any nation, state, ruler, business, or individual, the church also relativizes all merely human authority. This world belongs to God alone and to no one else.

The church is called to live according to the rules of the kingdom of God, but the church is not that kingdom. The purpose of the church is to be self-conscious about what that kingdom stands for and to model what that kingdom might look like. It is also the calling of the church to invite others to join in the work of God's kingdom. But it is not the church's role to rule.

Ever since the fourth century, when the Roman Empire adopted Christianity as its official state religion, Christian churches have had a complicated relationship with politics and government. Centuries of European history reveal a litany of intrigue between the church and the state. The era of Christendom, when the European Christian church was largely in control of both the culture and the state (from the fifth century to the seventeenth century), is remembered for its excesses: the Inquisition, the Crusades, and various witch hunts. The adage that power corrupts seems to apply within the church as much as outside it, and it was largely these abuses of power within the church that led to the emergence of the secular state in the seventeenth and eighteenth centuries.

Long before political power was wrested away from the church, however, numerous Christians had already become convinced that a healthy faith requires separation between church and state. The Anabaptists of the sixteenth century made this claim, as did many of the so-called free churches (meaning free from state control) that emerged in the seventeenth century and after. Many of the Europeans who migrated to America were motivated by a desire to organize churches that were free from government control and also free from the corrupting power of governing.

Christians continue to discuss the appropriate relationship between church and state. In his book *Christ and Culture,* the twentieth-century theologian H. Richard Niebuhr describes several options ranging from total separation to an almost complete merging with culture.[4] Some Christian groups remain separatistic (as, for example, the

♦ ♦

Should Christians become involved in politics? If so, in what ways? Is political partisanship always to be avoided? What special concerns should Christians bring to politics?

♦ ♦

Amish), while others are more willing to use government access to further Christian ideals. From the perspective of history, both the rise of democracy and the separation of church and state are recent developments. With only two centuries of experience, we still have much to learn concerning Christian citizenship in a democracy, and the church will surely be working on this issue for a long time to come.

Meanwhile, Christians need guidance about when, why, and how Christians should enter the political process. Present realities fall far short of what God intends for humankind and for creation as a whole. The church's role is not to defend things as they are but to speak as honestly as possible about the actual state of the world and then to work for change where change is needed.

The biblical scholar Walter Brueggemann makes the case that genuinely prophetic action on the part of the church—action that calls the kingdom of God into existence in a given society—will almost always spring from sorrow rather than from anger.[5] What moves us to civic action should be what makes us cry; our aching hearts should direct our concerns as Christians in the public sphere.

The public purpose of the church is prophetic: to feed the hungry, clothe the naked, care for the weary, and ask questions about why so many people are poor and naked and weary. The church is called to analyze the world politically, socially, and economically; to question current structures; and to propose new strategies of justice and compassion. In a real sense, the church is called to be a community of the never-satisfied-until-all-are-satisfied, a community with hope that the power of God's love can remake both our own lives and the shared life of the entire planet.

Worship

It is not always easy to feel the ache of compassion that God wants to place in our hearts. We are often too busy to pay attention to such matters, and sometimes we do not want to hear God's quiet voice reminding us of the world's sorrows. We need to stop and listen; we need to be reminded of who

God is and what God desires. Worship helps us in this task. In worship we present ourselves to God and ask God to remold our hearts and minds so that we can better see the world as God sees it, mourn for the world as God mourns for it, and ultimately love the world as God loves it.

Worship involves praise. We praise God as the Creator, and we praise God for being our Savior. Many Christians talk about praise as something we "give" to God, but the idea of giving worship or praise to God needs to be qualified. While God certainly deserves to be worshiped and sometimes even commands our worship, God does not *need* our worship any more than God *needs* anything else from us. What God asks from us in the way of worship is actually something that meets our own deep needs. In worship, as in so many other aspects of life, our attempt to give something to God results in God's giving much more to us.

Worship reminds us of the structure of the universe and our place in it. In that universe, God is at the center of all that exists. We have graciously been given a place in God's grand miracle of existence, but we are not the center. In corporate worship, surrounded as we are by others, we experience this self-decentering reality of being in God's presence. We are merely one among many others entering the presence of God, and God is the shared focus of everyone. Worship thus points us away from ourselves and reduces us to wonder over the fact that God is even mindful of our existence.

For many Christians, the central act of worship is the Eucharist or Holy Communion, a time when Christians share bread and wine just as Jesus did with his disciples at the Last Supper. The word *Eucharist* means thanksgiving, and the Eucharist is a feast of thanksgiving recalling the life, death, and resurrection of Jesus and making Christ present to us in the bread and wine. The Eucharist is also a symbol of all the good things God gives us: food and drink and friends to share them. It is a symbol of the way in which God feeds us spiritually, physically, socially, emotionally, and intellectually. The words of the service remind us that all heaven and earth are full of the glory of God and that all creation gives praise to God. In the Eucharist, we are part of something far bigger than ourselves, a foreshadowing of the great feast that will someday take place in heaven. It is a precursor of the time when God's bounty will overflow all bounds and God's grace will flood the universe.

> What experiences of worship do you find most meaningful? What do you think the purpose of worship should be? How important is the Lord's Supper or the Eucharist in your own life?

When we participate in worship, and especially in the Eucharist, we step outside ordinary time for a brief moment to a place where we catch a glimpse of the world as God sees it. When we leave worship to reenter ordinary time, we do so as changed people.

As individuals, we can worship God anywhere and anytime, but corporate worship provides a public rhythm to the Christian life. Worship starts, and it stops. Christian life is a repetitive cycle that moves back and forth constantly between worship and work. These two activities, worship and work, have been likened to spiritual breathing: What we inhale in worship we exhale in our work. The conclusion of corporate worship is, accordingly, a transition to work, and it typically ends with a commission like that found in the twelfth chapter of Romans (vv. 9–18):

> Let love be genuine; hate what is evil, hold fast to what is good; love one another with mutual affection; outdo one another in showing honor. Do not lag in zeal, be ardent in spirit, serve the Lord. Rejoice in hope, be patient in suffering, persevere in prayer. Contribute to the needs of the saints; extend hospitality to strangers. Bless those who persecute you; bless and do not curse them. Rejoice with those who rejoice, weep with those who weep. Live in harmony with one another; do not be haughty, but associate with the lowly; do not claim to be wiser than you are. Do not repay anyone evil with evil, but take thought for what is

noble in the sight of all. If it is possible, so far as it depends on you, live peaceably with all.

Such is the way of life that Christian worship is meant to encourage. We gather together for worship to be reminded of who we are, and we depart better equipped both to love God and to love everyone whom God places alongside us in our lives.

7

The Bible

The Bible is the Christian's great sourcebook, the one place where followers of Jesus turn repeatedly for guidance, consolation, encouragement, and hope. The Bible is an inspired book, revealing aspects of God's character that would otherwise be unknown. But the Bible is also a human book, assembled over hundreds of years, that documents how people have often stumbled their way through history, oblivious to God's care and concern.

These two aspects of the Bible, the human and the divine, are intertwined throughout the text, combined in the same stories, layered on top of each other. In that sense, the Bible is very much like life. The divine is present in the midst of human fallibility. We run across God in unexpected places and sometimes trip over God when we least expect to. Simultaneously, we sometimes discover sinners where we expect saints and saints where we anticipate finding sinners.

The Bible is an ancient and complex text that is not always easy to understand, but it is also our chief guide for Christian faith and life. How should we read this special book? What

do we mean when we say it is inspired and authoritative?
Why do Christians sometimes disagree about what it means?
What does the Bible communicate?

What Is the Bible?

While we call it a book, the Bible is not really a book in any
normal sense of that term. Instead, it is a library between two
covers, a remarkably diverse collection of writings composed
by many people in many times and settings. It is an eclectic
collection that took many hundreds of years to assemble,
but the items included are all there because they somehow
seemed necessary in order for the Bible's readers to develop
a full and proper understanding of God, the world, and what
it means to be human.

A homey analogy is to think of the Bible as something like
a refrigerator door in the kitchen of a large family. The door
is plastered with notes, messages, and mementos held on
by magnets or pieces of tape. Family pictures appear along
with grocery lists, clipped articles from the newspaper, and
announcements about various upcoming meetings (half of
which may already have taken place). There are coupons for
special sales, reminders that someone is on a diet, emergency
phone numbers, somebody's grade-school artwork, and perhaps some short and pithy comment spelled out with little
magnetic letters all lined up in a row. The mix may not make
sense to a visitor—it can look rather haphazard—but family
members can usually explain why most of it is there.

If that image seems too chaotic or irreverent, an alternative analogy is to liken the Bible to a newspaper. Just as a
newspaper includes many kinds of writing (front-page news,
ads, sports, fashion news, business reports, comics, editorials,
and local stories), so the Bible contains poetry, prose, snip-
pets of wisdom, laws, songs, stories, letters, philosophy, and
a variety of how-to advice. The different kinds of items that
appear in a newspaper require different kinds of background

knowledge and reading skills to make sense of them—reading the sports page is not at all like reading the classified advertisements—and the same applies to the Bible. Thus, biblical poetry is not supposed to be taken literally; it is meant to be read literarily. Letters contained in the Bible require a different kind of skill: the ability to read between the lines, where most of the important stuff in letters is usually found. The passages of the Bible that are written in the form of a stage play or drama (like Job and the book of Revelation) require still other interpretive skills.

One thing is for sure: The Bible reflects human life in all its good and bad complexity. Nothing is exempt from its pages. Its sinners sin boldly, and its saints pursue their saintly passions with exuberance and pleasure. The Bible describes treachery and hatred, but it also plumbs the depths of love and compassion. Every human experience or emotion is there—anger, beauty, alienation, arrogance, romance, tragedy, brutality, humor, sickness, and death. Its pages at times drip despair, but they can also ripple with hope and the sheer enjoyment of life lived well. It is all there, every facet of human existence.

> With which parts of the Bible are you most familiar? Have you ever read the entire Bible? Which parts of the Bible seem the hardest to understand?

What distinguishes the Bible, however, is that God is also there, sometimes in ways we expect and sometimes in ways that surprise or even trouble us. The Bible is a literary classic because of its portrayal of human existence, but it is a religious classic because it so wonderfully reveals God to us over and over again. The twentieth-century theologian Karl Barth said, "We shall always find in it as much as we seek and no more," but he added that "there is a river in the Bible that carries us away, once we have entrusted our destiny to it."[1]

That "river" derives from the Bible's inspired character; it springs from God's own presence within, behind, around, and in front of the text. But we need to be careful not to treat the Bible as a magical book. The Bible's inspired character has a specific purpose, as it was given "for teaching, for reproof, for correction, and for training in righteousness, so that everyone who belongs to God may be . . . equipped for every good work" (2 Tim. 3:16–17). The Bible does not provide esoteric knowledge hidden from other people. It is not a book of formulas designed to assure us of long life, good fortune, and wealth. Nor is it a book of science to explain the natural world. Instead, the Bible equips us for every good work. The Bible is given to make us better people, more fully in tune with God's deep affections for the world and the people who live in it.

✦✦✦✦✦✦✦✦✦✦✦✦✦✦✦✦✦✦✦✦✦✦✦✦✦✦✦✦✦✦✦✦✦✦✦✦✦

Sometimes the Bible simply reflects human life; sometimes it brings a new word from God. How do you tell the difference? Can meaning vary from person to person?

✦✦✦✦✦✦✦✦✦✦✦✦✦✦✦✦✦✦✦✦✦✦✦✦✦✦✦✦✦✦✦✦✦✦✦✦✦

Reading the Bible Intelligently

The Bible has much to tell us, but how do we unearth its messages and discover its treasures? At the time of the Protestant Reformation in the sixteenth century, some church leaders suggested that because the Bible is inspired by God it must also, by necessity, be easily understood. If the Bible is God's Word to us, they thought, its meaning must be easy to ascertain. If God wants us to live according to the Bible's message, its meaning should be right there on the surface.

This belief in the Bible's unambiguous clarity, which is called the perspicuity of Scripture, was used by Martin Luther and other Protestant Reformers to defend their new interpretations of the Bible against older medieval Catholic ways of explaining what the Bible said. In overly stark terms, the Catholic argument was that the Bible had to be read in the light of past tradition, that is, in agreement with the way earlier Christians had understood the Bible. The Protestant assumption was that past ways of reading the Bible could be in error: the only valid approach is to read each section of the Bible in light of its own simple and clear meaning and then compare text with text to see how they inform one another.

There is wisdom in both of these views but also danger. The strength of the traditional Catholic approach is that it necessarily links our reading of the Bible with the way Christians understood it in the past. This makes sense, since those who lived before us have much to teach us. Just because we are located later in history does not mean we are necessarily smarter or more spiritually insightful than our forebears. But reading the Bible only in light of past meanings can shut off the possibility of discovering new meaning and depth in Scripture.

In terms of the Protestant approach, there is great power in reading the Bible anew each time we sit down with it. What's more, some of the most important teachings of the Bible can be understood with relatively little interpretative effort. It does not require much hermeneutical finesse to understand that when Jesus said to forgive one another, he meant we are literally to forgive one another. When Jesus said to feed the hungry, clothe the naked, and give drink to the thirsty, we can pretty much assume he was talking about real people with real needs.

But the meaning of many other passages is harder to discern. What does the Bible mean when it says in the Ten Commandments that we should not kill, especially when some other passages seem to valorize horrendous acts of war? What does the Bible mean when it says in some passages that women should be silent in church but in others that men and women are equal in the Lord? How are we to interpret the powerful imagery found in the books of Daniel and Revelation? None of this is easy; none of it is unambiguously clear.

The nub of the problem is this: If we insist that the Bible is easy to understand, we will be prone to read our own ideas and views into the Bible because they will seem the most self-

◆◆◆◆◆◆◆◆◆◆◆◆◆◆◆◆◆◆◆◆◆◆◆◆◆◆◆◆◆◆◆◆◆◆

How easily is the Bible understood? Are some passages less clear than others? Has your devotional reading of the Bible ever raised questions that require scholarly research? Has your scholarly study of the Bible ever produced change in your faith?

◆◆◆◆◆◆◆◆◆◆◆◆◆◆◆◆◆◆◆◆◆◆◆◆◆◆◆◆◆◆◆◆◆◆

evident. Of course, when the meaning seems self-evident, it does not feel like we are interpreting the Bible at all; it feels like we are just reading what the Bible incontest-ably says. Too much confidence in our own reading can make us dogmatic when perhaps we should be humble, and presumptuous when we ought to be cautious. We need checks on the ways we interpret the Bible individually and even in groups. Some of these checks are found in tradition; some are found in reading the Bible in dialogue with people who have had different life experiences or come from different cultures (so that their sense of what is self-evident in the text can help us rethink what we see as self-evident); and some are found in the works of biblical scholars and theologians who devote their entire lives to understanding the Bible.

Intelligent reading of the Bible requires, on the one hand, making sense of individual passages of Scripture and, on the other hand, making sense of the message of the Bible as a whole. Most biblical scholars focus on the first task, seeking to decipher what specific passages of Scripture meant to the people to whom they were originally addressed. Most theologians focus on the second task, trying to integrate the many insights that are found in the Bible into a single overarching vision of God, the world, and humankind.

The Bible as a whole recounts the story of God's interactions with humanity, and that historical narrative has a progressive tone. Ideas develop. The plot thickens. The story line becomes more complex. God did not change in this process, but humanity's perception of God did. On some pages of the Bible, God seems to act like little more than a local tribal deity because that is how the people of that time imagined God.

Later, God is increasingly revealed as the creator of the entire universe, the lord of all creation. At one point, the rule of justice is an eye for an eye and a tooth for a tooth—no one is to exact more damage than they themselves have received—but later the standard is redefined in terms of forgiveness and nonretaliation. At some points, the Bible seems to condone the supremacy of men over women and to reinforce ethnic arrogance, but elsewhere the Bible says that all people, all men and all women from all the peoples of the world, are equal in God's sight.

While this biblical trajectory of development is not without its twists and turns, later passages in the Bible seem generally to expand or deepen the meanings of earlier passages. Thus, the special favor that God shows to Israel is ultimately expanded to include everyone, and older rules of tribal purity are slowly deepened into universally applicable norms of human moral behavior. As a result of such changes of insight, we no longer believe that slavery is allowable, that disobedient children should be stoned to death, or that women should be forbidden to cut their hair. Just because these sentiments appear in the Bible in one place or another does not mean they represent the Bible's last word on these topics.

The concept of progressive revelation is helpful in understanding the Bible, but it has to be used cautiously. Not everything is subject to development, and Christians generally agree that we should be leery of reading the Bible today in ways that are totally at odds with what those passages meant to the people for whom they were first written. The God we worship today is still the same God who was worshiped long ago by Abraham and Sarah and by Isaac and Jacob. Every book of the Bible, and every literary subunit, has its own integrity and its own messages to convey. Many of these messages are clear, but there is also much to take into account. It takes intelligence as well as a willing heart to read the Bible as the Christian's handbook of faith and guidebook for life.

The Church, the Churches, and the Bible

The earliest Christians—those who lived during the first fifty years or so of the Jesus movement—did not have the entire Bible available to them. The New Testament had not yet been gathered together; in fact, much of it had not yet been written. During those early years, Christians had to rely on the Old Testament, oral tradition handed down from Jesus and his disciples, the guidance of the Holy Spirit, and their own God-given powers of reason and judgment. Until the early 200s, most of the small Christian communities scattered around the Roman Empire possessed only some of the books that would later be incorporated into the New Testament. The Bible as we know it today came together following a long process of discernment about which writings seemed the most inspired by the Spirit, which were the most directly linked to Jesus and his disciples, and which seemed most needed by the church itself.

Not everyone has always been happy about those decisions, but the consensus of the church, especially about the twenty-seven books that form the canon of the New Testament, has been clear since at least the fourth century. For all the centuries since that time, Christians have had to take all of the Bible into account, even the parts we may not find particularly appealing. For example, Martin Luther, founder of the Protestant movement, really wished the book of James had not been included in the canon. Luther believed medieval Catholicism had overemphasized the role of human effort in Christian faith, and the book of James did not help him make his case. He thought that it placed too much emphasis on human effort and not enough on God's grace. But James is a part of the Bible, and therefore Luther had to deal with it. His own theology is stronger as a result.

Another example comes from the well-known African American preacher Howard Thurman. His concern—or, at least, his grandmother's concern—was with the writings of Paul. Thurman's grandmother had been a slave, and later in life she said she never wanted to read any of Paul's New Testament books again because some of Paul's writings had been used repeatedly to justify slavery and to tell slaves to be docile and obedient to their masters.[2] In contrast to Luther, she much preferred James to Paul. Her attitude is thoroughly understandable, but many spiritual treasures will be missed if Paul's writings are rejected because they have been used to do harm.

Scriptural preferences are also reflected in the history of Christian denominations. Different churches tend to emphasize different themes found in different books of the Bible and then to interpret the rest of the Bible in light of those themes, ironing out any interpretive wrinkles or difficult passages that get in the way. These favorite passages are sometimes referred to as a "canon within the canon." For example, Protestants in the Reformed tradition tend to take the book of Romans (especially the first eight chapters) as the key to the Bible as a whole, and they read the rest of the Bible through its Pauline, theologically systematic understanding of faith. Pentecostals often center on the book of Acts and read other passages of Scripture in light of that book's experiential emphases. Mennonites and other Anabaptists typically focus on the Gospels, especially the Sermon on the Mount, and then interpret other parts of the Bible in relation to its norms of compassion and peace. Other churches do the same thing with other themes derived from various passages within the Bible.

Through the years, these different ways of reading the Bible have supplied insight, wisdom, and instruction to a wide variety of individuals, churches, communities, and cultures. In the last century or so, these differences have become more evident, however, as we no longer live in isolation from one another but instead

♦♦♦♦♦♦♦♦♦♦♦♦♦♦♦♦♦♦♦♦♦♦♦♦♦♦♦♦♦♦♦♦♦♦

What passages of Scripture are most popular in your church? What passages seem to be overlooked or ignored? What is your own canon within the canon?

♦♦♦♦♦♦♦♦♦♦♦♦♦♦♦♦♦♦♦♦♦♦♦♦♦♦♦♦♦♦♦♦♦♦

rub shoulders every day. We can now communicate at will across denominational and cultural lines, becoming aware of one another's distinctives and strengths as well as peculiarities and shortcomings. Yet the Bible makes it clear that ultimately Jesus wants all his followers to be one, just as he and the Father are one (John 17:11).

It is this call to unity that prompted the modern ecumenical movement, which began in the early twentieth century for the purpose of promoting the visible unity of all Christians. No one expects that all Christians will agree on everything anytime soon. The goal is not to eliminate all differences of opinion and interpretation but to help one another evaluate what God is saying to us through the Bible. That means listening to one another with respect, learning from one another as much as we can, and living together in love as best we can.

In this ecumenical conversation about the Bible, Christians might find inspiration in the Jewish Talmud. The Talmud is a commentary on Scripture, and it has a unique format. Rather than propound the one right interpretation of a passage, the Talmud records a legacy of rabbinic debate about that text, with all the arguments, counterarguments, and counter-counterarguments displayed side-by-side on the page. As a result, the Talmud opens up conversation about a text rather than closing it down, and when Jews and others discuss the Talmud today, they join in that long legacy of religious debate about the Bible that the Talmud itself exemplifies.

Christians will never entirely agree about what the Bible says, but agreement is not the only thing that matters. The conversation itself is worthwhile, perhaps especially when we disagree. Our disagreements keep the Bible alive, forcing us to read it over and over again as carefully and as honestly as we can, letting the Bible speak to us rather than forcing our own meanings on to the text. Reading the Bible talmudic-style sharpens our understanding of the text while simultaneously calling us to respect and even love those with whom we disagree.

The Story and the Stories of the Bible

Despite the diversity that exists in Scripture, one overarching narrative holds the entire Bible together. This grand story of the Bible goes something like this: There was a time when nothing existed except God, and then God decided, purely out of love, to make something else. What God made is the reality in which we now live, the universe in all its vast and wonderful beauty. This universe is not a mere machine but instead is full of life. The life of humankind is uniquely stamped with God's own image, which includes both the freedom to love God and the freedom to turn away. Unfortunately, we often do turn away, trying to live on our own, oblivious to God's love and cut off from the real source of our existence. The world as we know it, with all its heartache and evil, is the result.

Despite humanity's failures, God's love for the world has been constant. The Bible explains that long ago God chose a covenant people, the Jews, to be a model for the rest of the world. God revealed the law to them and sent prophets to guide them into more profound understandings of God, themselves, and the world. God then entered history in the person of Jesus, taking on human form to communicate with us more clearly and to show us what true love looks like. Rather than heeding Christ's message, the world killed Jesus, but God raised him from the dead, honoring his life, affirming his message, and promising that someday the bonds of love that were meant to hold the world together would be fully restored. Even now, God is mending those bonds of love, reconciling us to God and one another. Someday that process will be complete. We do not know when or how that will happen, but someday, in some way, God will make all things new, and the whole of creation will be enveloped in God's love. We live in the middle of this grand narrative, and thus we cannot see clearly all the details of the story's beginning or its end, but we can discern the basic plot and understand its implications.

In addition to this grand story, the Bible also contains many other smaller stories. Some of these stories reflect the goodness of creation; others document humanity's freedom and failures. Some stories provide us with hope; others warn us not to presume about the future. Some stories deal with personal concerns; others are much more political in orientation. Some stories focus on lofty ideals; others address practical concerns. All these stories are important in their own right. They provide close-up views of life as it is: sometimes good, sometimes evil, sometimes sorrowful, and sometimes joyful.

◆◆◆◆◆◆◆◆◆◆◆◆◆◆◆◆◆◆◆◆◆◆◆◆◆◆◆◆◆◆◆◆◆◆◆◆

What is your favorite Bible story? What is its message for you? Why is it your favorite?

◆◆◆◆◆◆◆◆◆◆◆◆◆◆◆◆◆◆◆◆◆◆◆◆◆◆◆◆◆◆◆◆◆◆◆◆

One example of a story that has instructed Christians and Jews alike about goodness and evil is the tale of David and Bathsheba (2 Sam. 11:1–12:23). David is loved by God, but he is also a dismal sinner. He has a sexual encounter with Bathsheba, the wife of one of his soldiers, and when she becomes pregnant, David orders her husband to the front lines so he will be killed in battle. The Bible does not tone down the evil of this story but recounts it with blunt honesty. David and Bathsheba both suffer because of what has taken place. Their child dies. One of David's sons rises up against him and eventually is killed. Other revolts follow. His government is a mess. The story of David and Bathsheba demonstrates how severely we can damage both our own lives and the lives of others by our sin. It is a blunt warning to mind our ways.

The story of the wedding at Cana (John 2:1–10) records a very different kind of human encounter, one of joy, not evil. In this story, Jesus is attending a wedding feast when the wine runs out. The celebration is starting to unravel, and Jesus' mother asks him to do something. So Jesus makes more wine for the guests—really good wine, lots of wine—and the celebration gets back on track. What is the point? At least one message of this story is that there are times when it is fully appropriate to celebrate the goodness of life with exuberance. In particular, this story tells us that the pleasures of love and family are good and ought to be cherished.

The Bible deals with every facet of life and assures us that God cares about every moment. The Bible is simultaneously honest and hopeful, demanding and embracing, challenging and comforting. It offers us an awe-inspiring vision of God, a rich and complex portrayal of human life, and an unsurpassed body of wisdom for living. In helping us understand the breadth of human experience and the depth of God's grace, the Bible transforms us as we read it into persons ever more capable of showing grace to others.

8

The Future

Gracious Christianity is forward looking and hopeful. Someday, as Jesus taught us, God's kingdom will come in its fullness, and God's will really will be done on earth as it is in heaven. The path to that coming kingdom may not be as direct as we would like, and our present situation may sometimes be disturbing, but Christian hope is ultimately about long-term outcomes, not short-term optimism. Christian hope is about faithfully working together with God so that peace, righteousness, and justice are established on earth whenever possible, looking forward to the day when God will make all things new.

Talk about the future also raises questions about our own fates, not just the fate of the world as a whole. What will happen to us when we die? Will we see our loved ones again? Is there a heaven, and is there a hell? Just as important, how do our views about the future shape our attitudes and actions while we are still alive?

Realistic Hope

When speaking about the future, Christians are cautious about using the verb "to know." It is an awkward verb to pair with the future. We anticipate the future; we plan for the future; we speculate about the future; sometimes we worry about the future. But we cannot really *know* the future until it gets here. To speak about knowing the future is a bit like saying we can taste the color blue or smell the hardness of a rock. The grammar works, but the phrase itself does not make sense.

Although we cannot know the future, we can describe some of its characteristics. Most notably, God has promised a final triumph of good over evil and of love over hate. Consequently, Christians face the future with hope rather than with worry or fear. Like other people, we have legitimate concerns about our future health and happiness, but we also have a larger perspective that encompasses the prosperity and joy of the entire world.

We hope for peace, for justice, and for God's righteousness to be established on earth. We also hope that eventually we will be deemed worthy of citizenship in God's eternal kingdom, where love truly will define our affections for God and our concern for our neighbors.

What does it mean to be hopeful as a Christian? How is this similar to or different from optimism? How is hope related to faith and love?

This hopeful posture may, at times, be at odds with the dominant culture. In the ancient Roman Empire, most citizens feared the future. They worried that the gods were conspiring against them, eager to crush anyone who seemed too smug or too well off. So the Romans consulted the stars and analyzed the entrails of birds, trying to get a glimpse of the gods' devious plans in order to sidestep the traps that were being set. They grasped for any bit of knowledge that might enable them to outmaneuver the gods' ill will and to live long, healthy, and prosperous lives.

The attitude of their Christian neighbors was utterly different. Rather than feeling they needed to protect themselves from God's devious plans, the early Christians looked to God as their protector, comforter, lover, and friend. Rather than worrying about how to maximize their own wealth and status, Christians served others. Rather than thinking they could somehow outwit God, Christians freely admitted that God knew them better than they knew themselves and could not be tricked. So rather than worrying about what might happen, Christians trusted God and went about their daily tasks in peace.

Christians today possess that same trust, even though our subjective experience of hope may vary from day to day. Some days we feel closer to God and more secure in God's hands, and some days less so. Sometimes we feel upbeat about the prospects for peace and justice in our world; sometimes we do not. The world can regress as well as move ahead; there will be times of oppression as well as liberation. Hope is not always easy to maintain in the flux of life. In fact, hope is a virtue that needs to be cultivated in order to be kept alive. Even for Jesus there came a time when it was hard to hope: on the night of his arrest when he prayed in the Garden of Gethsemane that God would remove the cup from him and would spare him the agony of the cross (Mark 14:32–42).

How does your view of the future affect the way you live now? How does your view of God affect the way you think about the future? How should we pray and what should we pray for when we or others are suffering?

Jesus was not spared from the cross, and we will not avoid all the pain and suffering of life. Like everyone else, Christians will experience sickness and disease, the death of loved ones, the dissolution of friendships, the loss of jobs, the shattering of trust, the slander of enemies, the destruction that results from natural disasters, and the ravages of war. While miracles can happen, God does not usually hand out free tickets allowing us to bypass all the challenges of ordinary human existence. In the midst of trials and trouble, we remain hopeful because we trust that both our own lives and the final resolution of all things are ultimately in God's hands.

Praying and Working for God's Kingdom

Christians express hope through prayer, just as Jesus did in the prayer he taught his disciples as part of the Sermon on the Mount. The Lord's Prayer is recorded in two of the Gospels (Matt. 6:9–13; Luke 11:2–4), and the specific wording varies from church to church and translation to translation. Here are the traditional words of the Lord's Prayer from the King James Version of the Gospel of Matthew:

> Our Father which art in heaven, hallowed be thy name. Thy kingdom come. Thy will be done in earth, as it is in heaven. Give us this day our daily bread. And forgive us our debts, as we forgive our debtors. And lead us not into temptation, but deliver us from evil: For thine is the kingdom, and the power, and the glory, for ever. Amen.

The prayer of Jesus begins by expressing the desire for God's kingdom to come and God's will to be done on earth as it is in heaven. Then Jesus models how to pray for our own more immediate needs: to have enough food for each day, to be forgiven of our sins in the same way we forgive others, and to be spared from temptation and testing.

The Lord's Prayer approaches the future with a distinctive mix of patience and impatience. There is a tone of patience and contentment in the clauses that deal with our needs for daily sustenance, forgiveness, and freedom from temptation, but simultaneously, the Lord's Prayer sounds impatient when it speaks about God's kingdom. We want God's kingdom to come and God's will to be done on earth as soon as possible. In fact, the Beatitudes, which precede this prayer, say we are literally to hunger and thirst for *dikaiosune* (a Greek term that can be translated as both righteousness and justice). There is nothing patient about that kind of language.

It has been said that "when we pray 'Thy kingdom come' we are not making a request. We are taking a vow. We are pledging our willingness to allow God's kingdom to be established in and through us."[1] If we are not working to change the world so that it corresponds to what we request in prayer, then our prayers can hardly be considered heartfelt. Prayer is serious business, and working for God's kingdom—working to establish God's rule of love and justice in our hearts and in the lives of others—is urgent business that rightly makes us impatient.

Martin Luther King Jr. modeled this kind of holy impatience in his famous "Letter from a Birmingham Jail." In response to criticism from a group of northern white clergy who thought he was being overly confrontational in his quest for civil rights and was asking for too much justice much too quickly, King wrote:

> For years now I have heard the word "Wait!" It rings in the ear of every Negro with piercing familiarity. This "Wait" has almost always meant "Never." It has been a tranquilizing thalidomide, relieving the emotional stress for a moment, only to give birth to an ill-formed infant of frustration. We must come to see with the distinguished jurist of yesterday that "justice too long delayed is justice denied."[2]

Christians are called to holy impatience in their efforts to promote peace, righteousness, and justice. Like the prophets of old, we are to seek real change for real people in real time. But just as the Lord's Prayer mixes patience with impatience, we are also called to season our holy impatience with godly patience. If we fail to do this, we can easily become disappointed with ourselves and others and even with God, and that can lead to cynicism and despair.

Patience, however, comes in many forms. The kind of patience that leads to complacency is not helpful, but patience that strengthens us and reinvigorates us for the long-term work of God's kingdom is necessary and good. Martin Luther King Jr. denounced patience when it delayed justice, but he was fully aware that patience and endurance were needed if his work was to succeed. He is often quoted as saying that the arc of the moral universe is long, but it bends toward justice. Patience, seasoned with holy impatience, is what keeps us energized as we traverse that long arc.

◆◆◆◆◆◆◆◆◆◆◆◆◆◆◆◆◆◆◆◆◆◆◆◆◆◆◆◆◆◆◆◆◆◆◆◆◆◆

Have you ever felt you were being too patient in the face of injustice? Are there signals that tell us when to be more patient or less patient? Are Christians called to different levels of patience?

◆◆◆◆◆◆◆◆◆◆◆◆◆◆◆◆◆◆◆◆◆◆◆◆◆◆◆◆◆◆◆◆◆◆◆◆◆◆

The kingdom of God forms slowly in the world as each of us learns personally and together how to love God and one another more willingly, more fully, and more selflessly. The kingdom of God's righteousness is not something to be imposed on others; in fact, it cannot be imposed at all. As Christians, we have no delusions about the success of our efforts; we readily confess that God's kingdom will be fully completed only with the return of Christ.

Christians believe that Jesus will some day return to earth, but no one knows exactly when or how that will happen. If Christ's return is anything like the birth of Jesus, everyone will be surprised. No one expected the incarnation to happen the way it did, and it is highly unlikely that anyone has accurately guessed what God has in mind for the future.

When some people read the Bible, especially the book of Revelation, they think they can decipher a clear and detailed description of the end times in the fantastic symbolism of that book. Some people in every century have read Revelation as a blueprint of the future, convinced they knew exactly who the Antichrist was, when the great tribulation would begin, and much more. But they have all been proven wrong, and people making similar predictions today will almost certainly be proven wrong as well.

The Bible contains numerous reminders that we can never know the future in detail, and that applies to the return of

Christ as much as to any other subject. The book of Revelation is not intended to provide Nostradamus-like prophecy about future events. Its message is that no matter how bleak the situation may become, God ultimately will prevail, justice will be done, love will be victori-

Does your church hold strong views concerning how and when Christ will return? What do you think about such matters? Is it helpful to speculate about how history will end?

ous, and the powers of arrogance and evil that deform the world will be defeated once and for all. That is our reason for hope and our comfort in times of trouble.

Living and Dying

The previous chapter made a distinction between the grand story of the Bible and the many smaller stories it contains. A similar distinction applies to the future. So far we have been talking about the grand story of the future, but each of our own smaller, individual stories is also important. In fact, when we ponder our own death or the death of someone we love, our concern about the general fate of the world loses its intensity. We concentrate on the individual, and well we should. While God is deeply concerned about the world as a whole, God is equally interested in our own small but special lives, and God mourns with us when death comes near. The only time the Gospels record that Jesus wept is when he heard that his friend Lazarus had died.

Death is, however, unavoidable. It is a fact of life. It is a part of being mortal. But death still comes as a shock. Anyone who has had a foretaste of death or who lives under the shadow of a terminal disease knows the dread of leaving family and friends as well as the anxiety of feeling fragile and vulnerable. Awareness of one's own impending death is like a knife cutting through raw flesh, leaving its jagged awareness in every corner of our being. When death stalks, whether we are Christians or not, we feel its presence as an enemy knocking at the door.

We experience similar pain when death takes someone we love. The deep sorrow caused by separation from a loved one reveals how much we are defined by our relationships. In fact, in many ways we *are* our relationships, and when a loved one dies, a part of us literally dies with that person.

♦♦♦♦♦♦♦♦♦♦♦♦♦♦♦♦♦♦♦♦♦♦♦♦♦♦♦♦♦♦♦♦♦

What has helped you most when a loved one has died? Have you helped others who have suffered loss? Is it ever better to grieve alone?

♦♦♦♦♦♦♦♦♦♦♦♦♦♦♦♦♦♦♦♦♦♦♦♦♦♦♦♦♦♦♦♦♦

In an odd sense, however, the inescapability of death can also be perceived as a gift. The writer Anne Lamott says that "death is God's no to all human presumption."[3] That "no" can be comforting. When we contemplate our own deaths, it becomes apparent that everything does not depend on us. We can let go and trust the world to God and to those who survive us. We have work to do, but our work has its limitations. Others will pick up where we leave off; another generation will care for the world. Recognizing the limits of our lives gives us direction for the present.

Awareness of our own mortality is not always comforting, however. It has been said that "greed for life is what love for life becomes when it is limited by the fear of death."[4] Many people in the modern world find it hard not to be greedy for life. Ignoring the needs of others, they scramble frantically to fill up their own memory banks of experience before they die.

Hope for life beyond death and in the company of God dramatically alters a person's value system. It offers freedom from the mad rush to accumulate this-worldly experiences and encourages us to take time to be more gracious with friends, neighbors, family, and even strangers we meet along the way. This is God's good earth for us to enjoy with whatever depth of experience we can morally muster, but this is not our final destination.

During the days we live on earth, our job is to try to become the people we want to be for all eternity. That means understanding our calling in life and seeking to follow that calling as best we can, doing good and serving others. Death is not tragic; the tragedy is when people die with "commitments undefined, convictions undeclared, and service unfulfilled."[5]

Does reflecting on your own death make you more or less anxious to experience as much of life as possible? When observing others, is it possible to distinguish "greed for life" from "love for life"? Can you distinguish them in yourself?

Judgment, Heaven, and Hell

The belief in a final judgment has been a part of Christian teaching from the very beginning, and it has often been depicted in graphic, and sometimes goofy, detail. It is difficult to know what to make of these popular images of heaven and hell. Surely heaven will be much better than the pictures we have seen of harps and clouds and angel wings, and when it comes to hell, the imagery of underground fires and demons with pitchforks can seem equally cartoonish. What we do know is that our actions and attitudes in the present have long-range consequences for both ourselves and others, and the traditional symbols of heaven and hell point toward those consequences with dramatic, visceral power.

In terms of understanding God's final judgment on our lives, however, heaven and hell may not be the best place to begin. It may be better to ask what *final* judgment entails. What makes it final? Many contemporary theologians suggest that the finality of God's judgment on our lives has as much to do with its incontestability as with the time when it will take place. In other words, God's judgment is final because when it is rendered, whenever that may take place, we will know once and for all exactly who we are. In that moment of divine judgment, all pride will disappear and so will all false modesty. We will see ourselves as God sees us.

In the present, none of us is very good at judging ourselves. Some of us worry about every little thing we may have done wrong; others of us go through life largely oblivious to the good or evil we leave in our wake. We are obviously incapable of judging our own lives, and we are not likely to do a better job with others. What is more, Jesus said to refrain from judging. Judgment is God's work and never ours. The parable of the wheat and the weeds found in Matthew 13:24–30 reinforces this point. In this story, a field has been sown with both good seeds and weeds. As the tiny plants begin to grow, the farm workers, certain they can distinguish between the two, want to remove the weeds immediately. But the master says to leave the field alone until harvest, when the weeds can be removed without damaging the crop.

This parable reminds us that during our lives on earth none of us is ever in a position to spiritually judge our peers. We can never fully understand the challenges others face, nor can we know their hidden capacities for goodness or evil. We do not know what unexpected turns their lives may take, and we do not know what tragedies or blessings may befall them. In sum, our knowledge of others is so limited and our weaknesses are so encompassing that we are simply incapable of rendering any kind of fair

◆◆◆◆◆◆◆◆◆◆◆◆◆◆◆◆◆◆◆◆◆◆◆◆◆◆◆◆◆◆◆◆

When have you felt judged by other Christians? When have you judged others? What is the difference between judging and appropriate discernment?

◆◆◆◆◆◆◆◆◆◆◆◆◆◆◆◆◆◆◆◆◆◆◆◆◆◆◆◆◆◆◆◆

judgment at all. Instead of constantly evaluating the failures of others, we are called to forgive those failures, and instead of trying to pick all the small splinters of sin from our neighbor's eyes, we are told to concentrate on removing the logs of sin from our own (Matt. 7:1–5).

We still wonder, however, what will happen to us when we die and, in particular, what will happen to the obvious faults we possess? Few if any Christians live thoroughly holy lives. What happens to those imperfections when we die and face God's judgment?

Historically, Christians have given two rather different answers. The traditional Catholic view, in very simple form, is that God provides an experience or a place called purgatory. Those who have tried to love God and others but have not done so perfectly will have the sin "purged" from their lives so that they can stand before God in complete holiness. Purgatory is sometimes portrayed as a kind of antechamber to heaven, a place to stay until we are ready to enter God's presence without shame.

Protestants recognize the same reality as Catholics—that few if any of us are fully holy when we die—but traditionally, they have proposed a different scenario. Those who are entering heaven will have their remaining imperfections immediately covered over by Christ's holiness in the same way that clothing covers our nakedness. That borrowed, or imputed, holiness of Christ will eliminate any shame we might otherwise have felt in God's company, and we will experience perfect joy.

Both of these scenarios are speculative, but both are helpful in their own ways. Christians do not claim to be perfect. We know we are dependent on God's grace both in this life and the life to come, and we know that any holiness we possess either now or in the future is a gift from God. We do not know exactly what will take place after we die, but we know who will be in charge. It is the same gracious God who has already come to us in Jesus who will render final judgment on our lives—and if we know anything about God, it is that God is much more, not less, gracious and forgiving than we are.

The question of how God will judge us naturally brings up the issue of hell. What does the Bible's language of eternal punishment mean? Doesn't belief in hell contradict the graciousness we have ascribed to God over and over again in this book? This is a subject of lively debate within the Christian community. Christians agree that hell is separation from God

and from one another. Most also agree that hell is the result
of our unwillingness to embrace God's love much more than
it represents a limitation of God's grace. In Jesus' story about
the prodigal son (discussed in chap. 4), the older son meta-
phorically places himself in hell (i.e., separation) in relation
to his father because of the disdain he feels concerning the
grace bestowed on his younger brother. Embracing grace is
clearly the antithesis of hell.

Christian hope is, of course, much more concerned with
heaven than it is with hell. The Bible provides images of
heaven as a wedding celebration, a city made of jewels, a
banquet without end, and a realm where even animal enemies—lions and lambs—live peaceably together. C. S. Lewis
envisioned heaven as much more real than the world in
which we now live. In one of his works of fiction, he describes
newcomers to heaven as so weak and flimsy that initially the
grass pokes right through their feet, and only with time do
they grow as real as everything else around them.[6]

Many Christian writers have stressed that the central experience of heaven will be endless worship of God. Others
have emphasized relationships—that heaven will be a place
where relationships with loved ones will be restored forever
and where friendship with saints from every age will flourish.
Whatever the specific details, most Christians believe that
heaven promises a depth of holy pleasure that is currently
unimaginable. Our enjoyment of God will be intensified, as
will our enjoyment of one another, and every moment "will
be saturated with a joy that is undiminished by the thought
of its possible end."[7]

Christians cannot, of course, *know* the details of what happens after death. We do not know the future; it is all a matter
of hope. But that hope is not mere speculation. It springs from
the longings of our hearts, is grounded in assurances from the
Bible, and, most concretely, is based on the historical resurrection of Christ. Christians hope that we, like Jesus and because
of Jesus, will someday inhabit a new heaven and a new earth,
living in God's presence with all the saints forever.

With our future in the hands of a gracious God, we can relax. That does not mean we should become righteously lazy. There is plenty to do. God's will is clearly not yet being done on earth as it is in heaven. But as we pray and work for God's kingdom, and as we contemplate our own deaths, we can be assured that the future is in the hands of a God who loves us more than we love ourselves and who loves the entire world in the same way. That love is the source of all the grace we experience in our own lives, and it is the wellspring of the graciousness we seek to show to others.

Conclusion

G race is at the core of the Christian gospel. We are by no means the first people to come to this conclusion. Many others have said it before. One of the most articulate was Johann Arndt, who lived around 1600. Arndt was a Lutheran minister whose preaching was set amid the religious violence that convulsed Europe for almost a century following the Protestant Reformation. Catholics and Protestants tried to silence one another, and Protestants and Catholics together sought to crush the religious revolutionaries known as Anabaptists. Violence was rampant in the streets. Churches were destroyed. Children were sometimes taken from their families. People were killed for their beliefs.

In the midst of revolution bordering on anarchy, Arndt published a volume entitled *True Christianity*. He argued that the essence of true Christianity, the characteristic that indicated whether or not anyone, Protestant or Catholic, was truly Christian, was "nothing else except service given to neighbor with love and pleasure."[1] For Arndt, serving others with love *and pleasure* was the indicator of Christian character. His description of Christianity represented a stunning break with the culture of his day and stood in contrast to the aggressive dogmatism that defined so many of the churches of the day, including his own beloved Lutheran Church.

It is important to note that, for Arndt, love of neighbor was inseparably linked with love of God. As he put it, "The love of God and the love of neighbor are one thing and must not be divided."[2] If we genuinely love others, we are in some sense also loving God. If we genuinely love God, we will find that we also necessarily love others. Arndt reminded his contemporaries that this is what Jesus commanded us to do. This is the creed of Jesus; this is the Christian's rule of life. This is gracious Christianity.

Gracious Christianity is not a new kind of faith. It is not another new version of Christianity that sees itself as better than, or in competition with, other church traditions. It is part of our common heritage and part of our common hope. Gracious Christianity is the nub of what C. S. Lewis called "mere Christianity," the convictions that have been "common to nearly all Christians at all times."[3] Mere Christianity does not deal with everything that can be said about a particular theological subject; such a degree of detail has to be worked out by each church on its own. Rather, Lewis likened this common core of faith to the hallway of a large guest house. The people who live in the house share the hallway, even though they reside in their own particular rooms. Similarly, Christians reside in their own particular congregations and denominations where they are nurtured and sustained in Christian faith, yet they share a hallway of common commitments and beliefs.

Whether Baptist or Catholic, Methodist or Pentecostal, Presbyterian or Mennonite, Orthodox or Anglican, as mere Christians we share a common calling to serve our neighbors with love and pleasure. As gracious Christians, we are called to be people of steadfast conviction as well as people of welcome and embrace. We are called to be people of high moral courage as well as people who refuse to judge. We are called to be people of deep spiritual devotion as well as people who understand the earthly needs of those around us.

As Christians, every one of us participates in a story of grace received and grace re-gifted to others. It is that ongoing cycle of grace that defines gracious Christianity. We need one another's help to keep that cycle going, and we need a framework of Christian ideas to remind us why we ought to be gracious to everyone, to our enemies as well as to our friends. In the end, however, it is living itself that matters, and we hope this book in some small way helps followers of Jesus to better live the love we profess.

> For small group study materials,
> teaching aids, and other resources,
> see www.graciouschristianity.org.

Notes

Introduction

1. Scot McKnight, *The Jesus Creed: Loving God, Loving Others* (Brewster, MA: Paraclete Press, 2004), 11.

2. Rick Warren, *The Purpose Driven Life: What on Earth Am I Here For?* (Grand Rapids: Zondervan, 2002), 125.

3. Marcus Borg, *Reading the Bible Again for the First Time* (San Francisco: HarperSanFrancisco, 2001), 301–2.

4. See Brian McLaren, *A Generous Orthodoxy* (Grand Rapids: Zondervan, 2004).

Chapter 1: God and Creation

1. *The Larger Catechism of the Westminster Assembly* (Philadelphia: Presbyterian Church, 1923), 3.

2. On the relationship between faith and academic study in general, see Douglas Jacobsen and Rhonda Hustedt Jacobsen, *Scholarship and Christian Faith: Enlarging the Conversation* (New York: Oxford University Press, 2004).

3. Karl Barth, *The Word of God and the Word of Man* (New York: Harper & Row, 1957), 24.

4. Augustine, *The Trinity,* trans. Edmund Hill, ed. John E. Rotelle (Brooklyn: New City Press, 1991). See especially books 8 and 9.

5. Dorothy Sayers, *Creed or Chaos?* (Manchester, N.H.: Sophia Institute Press, 1949), 22–23.

Chapter 2: Human Nature

1. See Abraham Cohen, *Everyman's Talmud: The Major Teachings of the Rabbinic Sages* (New York: Schocken Books, 1949), 214.

2. Kenneth Cain Kinghorn, ed., *John Wesley on the Sermon on the Mount: The Standard Sermons in Modern English,* vol. 2 (Nashville: Abingdon, 2002), 255.

3. Evelyn Underhill, *The School of Charity* (1934; repr., Harrisburg, PA: Morehouse, 1991), 11.

4. Charles M. Coffin, ed., *The Complete Poetry and Selected Prose of John Donne* (New York: Random House, 1952), 441.

5. Ernest L. Boyer, *Selected Speeches, 1979–1995* (Princeton: Carnegie Foundation for the Advancement of Teaching, 1997), 12.

6. Thomas Massaro, *Living Justice: Catholic Social Teaching in Action* (Lanham, MD: Sheed & Ward, 2000), 19–20.

7. Catherine of Sienna, *The Dialogue*, trans. Suzanne Noffke (New York: Paulist Press, 1980), 35.

8. Quoted in Johann Christoph Arnold, *Why Forgive?* (Farmington, PA: Plough Publishing House, 2000), front material.

Chapter 3: Hearing God's Voice

1. Lesslie Newbigin, *Proper Confidence: Faith, Doubt, and Certainty in Christian Discipleship* (Grand Rapids: Eerdmans, 1995), 105.

2. Gerard Manley Hopkins, *Poems of Gerard Manley Hopkins*, 3rd ed. (New York: Oxford University Press, 1948), 70.

3. Thomas Aquinas, *Summa Contra Gentiles*, vol. 1, trans. Anton C. Pegis (Notre Dame: University of Notre Dame Press, 1975). See especially chapter 13 of book 1.

4. Frederica Mathewes-Green, *At the Corner of East and Now* (New York: Jeremy P. Tarcher/Putnam, 2000), 4–5.

5. *Catechism of the Catholic Church*, 2nd ed. (New York: Doubleday, 1995), 673–74.

6. Desmond Tutu, *God Has a Dream* (New York: Doubleday, 2004), 71.

Chapter 4: The Fullness of Salvation

1. Walter Rauschenbusch, *A Theology for the Social Gospel* (Nashville: Abingdon, 1945), 99.

2. Henri J. M. Nouwen, *The Wounded Healer* (New York: Doubleday, 1979), 76.

3. Leonardo Fernando and G. Gispert-Sauch, *Christianity in India* (New York: Penguin, 2004), 53–54.

Chapter 5: The Spirit and Life

1. Gerald Sittser, *The Will of God as a Way of Life* (Grand Rapids: Zondervan, 2000), 29.

2. G. E. H. Palmer, Philip Sherrard, and Kallistos Ware, eds. and trans., *The Philokalia: The Complete Text*, vol. 4 (London: Faber & Faber, 1995), 58.

3. Dietrich Bonhoeffer, *The Cost of Discipleship* (New York: Macmillan, 1963), 99.

4. Ibid., 100.

5. Ibid., 335.

6. Kent Nerburn, *Make Me an Instrument of Your Peace: Living in the Spirit of the Prayer of St. Francis* (San Francisco: HarperSanFrancisco, 1999), front material.

Chapter 6: Being Church

1. Anne Lamott, *Traveling Mercies: Some Thoughts on Faith* (New York: Pantheon Books, 1999), 103.

2. See Philip P. Hallie, *Lest Innocent Blood Be Shed: The Story of the Village of Le Chambon and How Goodness Happened There* (New York: Harper & Row, 1979).

3. Frederick Douglass, "The Narrative of the Life of Frederick Douglass, an American Slave, Written by Himself," in *The Oxford Frederick Douglass Reader*, ed. William L. Andrews (New York: Oxford University Press, 1996), 93.

4. H. Richard Niebuhr, *Christ and Culture* (New York: Harper & Row, 1951).

5. Walter Brueggemann, *The Prophetic Imagination* (Minneapolis: Fortress, 1978). See especially chapter 3, "Prophetic Criticism and the Embrace of Pathos."

Chapter 7: The Bible

1. Karl Barth, *The Word of God and the Word of Man* (New York: Harper & Row, 1957), 32, 34.

2. Howard Thurman, *Jesus and the Disinherited* (Richmond, ID: Friends United Press, 1981), 30–31.

Chapter 8: The Future

1. James Mulholland, *Praying Like Jesus: The Lord's Prayer in a Culture of Prosperity* (San Francisco: HarperSanFrancisco, 2001), 53.

2. Martin Luther King Jr., *I Have a Dream: Writings and Speeches That Changed the World,* ed. James M. Washington (San Francisco: HarperSanFrancisco, 1986), 87–88.

3. Anne Lamott, *Traveling Mercies: Some Thoughts on Faith* (New York: Pantheon Books, 1999), 92.

4. Richard Bauckham and Trevor Hart, *Hope against Hope: Christian Eschatology at the Turn of the Millennium* (Grand Rapids: Eerdmans, 1999), 206.

5. Ernest L. Boyer, "Making Connections" (originally presented in March 1993), in *Selected Speeches, 1979–1995* (Princeton: Carnegie Foundation for the Advancement of Teaching, 1997), 116.

6. C. S. Lewis, *The Great Divorce* (New York: Macmillan, 1946), 19, passim.

7. Miroslav Volf, "Enter into Joy: Sin, Death, and the Life of the World to Come," in *The Ends of the World and the Ends of God: Science and Theology on Eschatology,* ed. John Polkinghorne and Michael Welker (Harrisburg, PA: Trinity Press International, 2000), 278.

Conclusion

1. Johann Arndt, *True Christianity,* trans. Peter Erb (New York: Paulist Press, 1979), 133.

2. Ibid., 126.

3. C. S. Lewis, *Mere Christianity* (San Francisco: HarperSanFrancisco, 2001), viii.

Index